MW00762590

For my Dear
Mike,

Over these many yrs
we have had many fun
experiences + adventures) -
So many stories) to tell.
Hope you enjoy the one
on page 163.

Love you,
Joanne

Hot Chocolate for Seniors

More than 100 heartwarming, humorous, inspiring stories written by seniors, for seniors, and about seniors!

Compiled by

Jan Fowler,

Author/Editor

BALBOA.
PRESS

A DIVISION OF HAY HOUSE

Copyright © 2011 Jan Fowler.

All rights reserved. No part of this book may be used or reproduced by any means, graphic, electronic, or mechanical, including photocopying, recording, taping or by any information storage retrieval system without the written permission of the publisher except in the case of brief quotations embodied in critical articles and reviews.

ISBN: 978-1-4525-3945-4 (sc)
ISBN: 978-1-4525-3944-7 (e)
ISBN: 978-1-4525-3946-1 (hc)
Library of Congress Control Number: 2011916715

Balboa Press books may be ordered through booksellers or by contacting:

Balboa Press
A Division of Hay House
1663 Liberty Drive
Bloomington, IN 47403
www.balboapress.com
1-(877) 407-4847

Because of the dynamic nature of the Internet, any web addresses or links contained in this book may have changed since publication and may no longer be valid. The views expressed in this work are solely those of the author and do not necessarily reflect the views of the publisher, and the publisher hereby disclaims any responsibility for them.

Any people depicted in stock imagery provided by Thinkstock are models, and such images are being used for illustrative purposes only.
Certain stock imagery © Thinkstock.

Printed in the United States of America

Balboa Press rev. date: 11/01/2011

∝ WITH GRATITUDE ∞

There are always special people on the sidelines who form the "cheering squad." For as many seasons as it takes to reach the goal, they cheer you on with enthusiastic love and support. My loyal supporters have been my wonderful family, *Janelle, Andy, Scott, and Mitchell Woodward; Dr. Kristen, Dr. Larry, and Lorenzo Fiorentino; Randy, Kel, Sophia, and Della Schmitz;* and *David Weir* for his enduring friendship and love. All have been a continuing source of joy to me over the years and I appreciate and love them dearly.

❧ Dedication ❧

This book is lovingly dedicated to you, the reader, and to seniors everywhere. Won't you laugh with me, cry with me, sing and smile with me as you turn the pages of this book? Life is a song so my wish for you is that you do the things that makes your heart sing. There's still so much magic left in life for us all to discover and enjoy.

❧ Preface ❧

Just make mine chocolate!

Who said you must be a chunk of cheese, bottle of wine, or keg of beer to improve with age? Why, we seniors do it all the time! In fact, we have a unique character of our own, all smoothed and honeyed by the passage of time. Like precious gems, we comprise an elite genre of society with an immense wealth of talent and experience to offer the world. Are you aware of just how many of our world's most accomplished people are over sixty? Not only do we seniors have a lot to offer, but as today's aging population, we can still pack a dazzling, powerful punch.

Just think, Ronald Reagan was nearly seventy when elected president of the United States, and served until he was seventy-seven. Winston Churchill was sixty-two when he became prime minister of England. Julia Childs was still writing best-selling cookbooks and demonstrating her mouth-watering French cuisine recipes on TV until she was well into her eighties. Astronaut and U.S. Senator John Glenn was shot into outer space a second time at age seventy-seven. California Governor Jerry Brown returned to office for a third term at seventy-three, and at eighty-nine, actress and show biz personality Betty White continues to dazzle us in the entertainment world. These are but a few shining examples of "seniors with sizzle." The list goes on and on . . . If you don't believe me, just look around. We still rock!

But unfortunately, we happen to live in a youth-obsessed culture that makes it all too easy to fall into a "senior slump," a state of mind in which we feel all washed up or begin believing we're too old to try something new. The truth is, we become old when we're lulled into settling for a quiet, passive life and *stop* inviting new challenges. But if we tell ourselves we feel strong, vibrant, and are still smart enough at problem-solving—especially when baffled by all the new technology—we're far more likely to exude good health, happiness, and prosperity.

And we seniors still have dreams to fulfill. Many of us haven't even seen our greatest victories yet. As a matter of fact, it wasn't till I reached my mid-sixties that my life really began to take off and my glorious odyssey began. I became a national columnist with two million readers, plus a speaker and television producer/host—things I had never dared to dream of doing when I was younger.

This season in life is also meant to be fun. Some days I feel wrapped in silk as I overflow with gratitude for my abundant happiness, loving friendships, good health, and joy received from taking part in FUN activities centered around community, church, volunteerism, children, grandchildren, and my speaking and writing career as an ambassador for seniors.

And finally, regarding the title of this anthology . . . I believe that one day it will be scientifically proven that chocolate is the answer to world peace. Oh, the wondrous, magical benefits of chocolate! Chocolate touches the heart, soothes the soul, arouses our taste buds, and even boosts our energy level. So wherever we are in this chocolate experience—be it dark, milk, white, powdered, syrup, or hot fudge topping—*please*, just make mine chocolate!

❧ Acknowledgments ☙

I happen to be a strong believer in group energy, so I took it upon myself to hand-pick three of the finest "rocket-booster" colleagues I could possibly find for my "Dream Team." The value of a Dream Team is that when you surround yourself with people *you* love who also love *you*, you'll get the lifting power you need. After all, even the most optimistic person in the world needs encouragement from time to time.

My talented Dream Team members were Susan Ullrich, my associate television producer; Kam Kalanui, my television production coordinator; and Shirley Huston, my director of marketing and literary agent/editor. All became trusted friends and capable advisors who always sought the best for me. The four of us met regularly each Wednesday at noon (I always provided them with lunch). And it wasn't long before our meetings became so exciting that they turned into celebrations, with sparks of enthusiasm turbo-charging the air the minute they burst through the door, unable to contain their latest success or accomplishment with one or more aspects of Jan Fowler Senior Productions!

Soon my team grew to include the remarkable talents of a prestigious editorial staff, as well: Bruce McAllister, award-winning author, English professor emeritus, and book coach; Mike Foley, magazine editor/writer, and university writing instructor; Bobbe Monk, newspaper writer/editor with more than fifty years' experience in journalism; Stephen Baetge, newspaper and magazine editor/journalist; and Karla Trosper, permissions editor, whose impressive skills to "get through" to the right person stem from her extensive marketing talents.

☙ SPECIAL MENTION ❧

Others who encouraged and inspired me along the way were Judy Rogers, Anne Sandel, Fran Gambino, Pat and Dan Damon, Norah Figueroa, Joan van Ommen, Connie Jury, Cheryl Flynn, Terri Guaglione, Lucille Caia, Inessa Niks, Amanda Secola (publisher/editor of *Not Born Yesterday!*), and my faithful Pen Women sisters

I was also cheered on by the highly-spirited fun-loving Ellen Schouest, Lisa Layton, Cher Sadler, Barbara Park, Trish Wyper, Suzanne Owens, Anne Jackson, Amy Kamiyama, Sue McCluskey, Felice Brezsny, Kristy Parr, Martha Brossia, and Helen Donovan—all of whom share "The Divine Secrets of the La-La Sisterhood" and whose lips remain forever sealed.

On a more heavy-hearted note, I wish to honor the memory of the winsome Stephen Baetge, who served as editor-in-chief of *Spectrum* (Sacramento, CA) which published my columns weekly, for his years of humorous good-natured banter, guidance, encouragement, and support of this work.

Most especially, I thank my wonderful contributing authors from the bottom of my heart for sharing their personal true-life stories. I send each one special love for they have done what we all must do—leave written memories as a legacy for our families to enjoy. Doing so helps fill the empty spaces in our hearts.

I will always be appreciative of my many wonderful television guests who graciously shared their valuable tips and insights for senior living and who applauded me for *Hot Chocolate for Seniors* before it was even *started*! Among these loyal supporters was eighty-eight-year-old Juanita Kelly who always called at the "precise moment" when I needed a lift during my arduous two-year book-writing journey.

And where would I ever be without the cheerful dependability and quality editorial services of Susan Snowden? Susan has the eye of an eagle. No detail ever escapes her attention. (www.snowdeneditorial.com).

I am also grateful for the many computer "rescue missions" and amazing wizardry of Dimitri Niks, Jim Johnson, Doug Wilson, Russ Dalton, Steven Wise, and Kevin Brennan and Mike Riddle at Inland Empire Computers www.inlandempirecomputers.com.

My thanks to publishing guru Dan Poynter for carrying several calls for story submissions for this book in his monthly newsletters and for always answering my questions, no matter where he happened to be in the world (http://ParaPublishing.com.)

My deep appreciation also goes to Bob Marckini for inviting readers of his monthly Proton Cancer Treatment newsletter to submit stories for my book (www.protonbob.com or RMarckini@protonbob.com)

I will always be grateful for the "effervescent" loyalty and enduring friendships of Barbara Berg, Melanie Fleming, Andrea Giambrone, Jackie Goldberg ("The Pink Lady"), Kathleen Ronald, and Gloria Loring—all of whom were "razzle-dazzle" keynote speakers for Starburst Inspirations, my nonprofit corporation which supports Drug Court. I thank them all for their encouragement and unfaltering faith in my ability to reach my goals.

I also extend great appreciation to my loving sparkling high-voltage "spirit sisters", Joanna Mersereau, Katie Robinson, Edelgard Schweitzer, Nan Sherman, Rebecca Gibson, and Sharon Kauffman, who enlarged my vision each week by filling me with beauty and sunshine from their souls.

And lastly, my deepest appreciation goes to the brilliant, talented, and delightfully entertaining Paul Ryan, my television hosting coach at CBS, who inspired the idea for this book in the first place.

❦ CONTENTS ❧

Chapter 2: Falling in Love Again   29

Chapter 3: Animal Blessings   59

Chapter 6: Hot Dogs & Mustard for Sports Fans   135

Chapter 7: Spit, Feathers, & Other Humorous Philosophies   153

Chapter 1:
ANGELS' WINGS & OTHER
UNEXPLAINED MYSTERIES

The Wallet

by Arnold Fine

As I stumbled home one freezing day, I happened upon a wallet someone had lost in the street. I picked it up and looked inside to find some identification so I could call the owner. But the wallet contained only three dollars and a crumpled letter that looked as if it had been in there for years.

The envelope was worn and the only thing that was legible on it was the return address. I started to open the letter, hoping to find some clue. Then I saw the date—1924. The letter had been written almost sixty years earlier.

It was written in a beautiful feminine handwriting on powder-blue stationery with a little flower in the left-hand corner. It was a "Dear John" letter that told the recipient, whose name appeared to be Michael, that the writer could not see him anymore because her mother forbade it. Even so, she wrote that she would always love him. It was signed Hannah.

It was a beautiful letter, but there was no way, except for the name Michael, to identify the owner. Maybe if I called information, the operator could find a phone listing for the address on the envelope.

"Operator," I began, "this is an unusual request. I'm trying to find the owner of a wallet that I found. Is there any way you can tell me if there is a phone number for an address that was on an envelope in the wallet?"

She suggested I speak with her supervisor, who hesitated for a moment, then said, "Well, there is a phone listing at that address, but I can't give you the number." She said that as a courtesy she would call that number, explain my story, and ask whoever answered if the person wanted her to connect me. I waited a few minutes and then the supervisor was back on the line. "I have a party who will speak with you."

I asked the woman on the other end of the line if she knew anyone by the name of Hannah. She gasped. "Oh! We bought this house from a family who had a daughter named Hannah. But that was thirty years ago!"

"Would you know where that family could be located now?" I asked.

"I remember that Hannah had to place her mother in a nursing home some years ago," the woman said. "Maybe if you got in touch with them, they might be able to track down the daughter."

She gave me the name of the nursing home, and I called the number. The woman on the phone told me the old lady had passed away some years ago, but the nursing home did have a phone number for where the daughter might be living.

I thanked the person at the nursing home and phoned the number she gave me. The woman who answered explained that Hannah herself was now living in a nursing home.

This whole thing is stupid, I thought to myself. *Why am I making such a big deal over finding the owner of a wallet that has only three dollars and a letter that is almost sixty years old?*

Nevertheless, I called the nursing home in which Hannah was supposed to be living, and the man who answered the phone told me, "Yes, Hannah is staying with us."

Even though it was already 10 p.m., I asked if I could come by to see her. "Well," he said hesitatingly, "if you want to take a chance, she might be in the day room watching television."

I thanked him and drove over to the nursing home. The night nurse and a guard greeted me at the door. We went up to the third floor of the large building. In the day room, the nurse introduced me to Hannah. She was a sweet silver-haired old-timer with a warm smile and a twinkle in her eye.

I told her about finding the wallet and showed her the letter. The second she saw the powder-blue envelope with that little flower on the left, she took a deep breath and said, "Young man, this letter was the last contact I ever had with Michael."

She looked away for a moment, deep in thought, and then said softly, "I loved him very much. But I was only sixteen at the time and my mother felt I was too young. Oh, he was so handsome. He looked like Sean Connery, the actor.

"Yes," she continued, "Michael Goldstein was a wonderful person. If you should find him, tell him I think of him often. And," she hesitated for a moment, almost biting her lip, "tell him I still love him. You know," she said, smiling as tears welled up in her eyes, "I never did marry. I guess no one ever matched up to Michael . . ."

I thanked Hannah and said good bye. I took the elevator to the first floor and as I stood by the door, the guard there asked, "Was the old lady able to help you?"

I told him she had given me a lead. "At least I have a last name. But I think I'll let it go for a while. I spent almost the whole day trying to find the owner of this wallet."

I had taken out the wallet, which was a simple brown leather case with red lacing on the side. When the guard saw it, he said, "Hey, wait a minute! That's Mr. Goldstein's wallet. I'd know it anywhere with that bright red lacing. He's always losing that wallet. I must have found it in the halls at least three times."

"Who's Mr. Goldstein?" I asked, as my hand began to shake.

"He's one of the old-timers on the eighth floor. That's Mike Goldstein's wallet for sure. He must have lost it on one of his walks."

I thanked the guard and quickly ran back to the nurse's office. I told her what the guard had said. We went back to the elevator and got on. I prayed that Mr. Goldstein would be up.

On the eighth floor, the floor nurse said, "I think he's still in the day room. He likes to read at night. He's a darling old man."

We went to the only room that had any lights on, and there was a man reading a book. The nurse went over to him and asked if he had lost his wallet. Mr. Goldstein looked up with surprise, put his hand in his back pocket, and said, "Oh, it *is* missing!"

"This kind gentleman found a wallet and we wondered if it could be yours."

I handed Mr. Goldstein the wallet, and the second he saw it, he smiled with relief and said, "Yes, that's it! It must have dropped out of my pocket this afternoon. I want to give you a reward."

"No, thank you," I said. "But I have to tell you something. I read the letter in the hope of finding out who owned the wallet."

The smile on his face suddenly disappeared. "You read that letter?"

"Not only did I read it, I think I know where Hannah is."

He suddenly grew pale. "Hannah? You know where she is? How is she? Is she still as pretty as she was? Please, please tell me," he begged.

"She's fine . . . just as pretty as when you knew her," I said softly.

The old man smiled with anticipation and asked, "Could you tell me where she is? I want to call her tomorrow." He grabbed my hand and said, "You know something, mister? I was so in love with that girl that when that letter came, my life literally ended. I never married. I guess I've always love her."

"Michael," I said, "come with me."

We took the elevator down to the third floor. The hallways were darkened and only one or two little night lights lit our way to the day room, where Hannah was sitting alone, watching the television.

The nurse walked over to her.

"Hannah," she said softly, pointing to Michael, who was waiting with me in the doorway. "Do you know this man?"

She adjusted her glasses, looked for a moment, but didn't say a word.

Michael said softly, almost in a whisper, "Hannah, it's Michael. Do you remember me?"

She gasped. "Michael! I don't believe it! Michael! It's you! My Michael!"

He walked slowly toward her, and they embraced. The nurse and I left with tears streaming down our faces.

"See," I said. "See how the good Lord works! If it's meant to be, it will be."

About three weeks later, I got a call at my office from the nursing home. "Can you break away on Sunday to attend a wedding? Michael and Hannah are going to tie the knot!"

It was a beautiful wedding, with all the people at the nursing home dressed up to join in the celebration. Hannah wore a light beige dress and looked beautiful. Michael wore a dark blue suit and stood tall. They made me their best man.

The hospital gave them their own room, and if you ever wanted to see a seventy-six-year-old bride and a seventy-nine-year-old groom acting like two teenagers, you had to see this couple.

A perfect ending for a love affair that had lasted nearly sixty years.

Reprinted with the kind permission of Arnold Fine, © 1998 **Arnold Fine**.

Arnold Fine is a writer, educator, newspaper and magazine journalist and photographer whose career spanned more than fifty years. He was also a teacher and coordinator for brain-injured children at Samuel J. Tilden High School in Brooklyn, NY. Now retired, he lives in Lower Manhattan.

Protected by Prayer

by Cheri Fuller

The missionary rose and prepared to leave the campsite where he had spent the night en route to the city for medical supplies. He extinguished his small campfire, pulled on his canvas backpack, and hopped on his motorcycle to continue his ride through the African jungle. Every two weeks he made this two-day journey to collect money from a bank and purchase medicine and supplies for the small field hospital where he served. When he completed those errands, he hopped on his bike again for the two-day return trip.

When the missionary arrived in the city, he collected his money and medical supplies and was just about to leave for home when he saw two men fighting in the street. Since one of the men was seriously injured, the missionary stopped, treated him for his injuries, and shared the love of Christ with him. Then the missionary began his two-day trek home, stopping in the jungle again to camp overnight.

Two weeks later, as was his custom, the missionary again made the journey to the city. As he ran various errands, a young man approached him—the same man the missionary had ministered to during his previous trip. "I knew you carried money and medicine with you," the man said, "so my friends and I followed you to your campsite in the jungle after you helped me in the street. We planned to kill you and take all the money and drugs. But just as we were about to move in and attack you, we saw twenty-six armed guards surround and protect you."

"You must be mistaken," said the missionary. "I was all alone when I spent the night in the jungle. There were no guards or anyone else with me."

"But, sir, I wasn't the only one who saw the guards. My five companions saw them too. We counted them! There were twenty-six bodyguards, too many for us to handle. Their presence stopped us from killing you."

Months later, the missionary related this story to the congregation gathered at his home church in Michigan. As he spoke, one of the men listening stood up and interrupted him to ask the exact day the incident in the jungle had occurred. When the missionary identified the specific month and day of the week, the man told him "the rest of the story."

"On the exact night of your incident in Africa, It was morning here in Michigan, and I was on the golf course. I was about to putt when I felt a strong urge to pray for you. The urge was so strong that I left the golf course and called some men of our church right here in this sanctuary to join me in praying for you. Would all you men who prayed with me that day stand up?"

The missionary wasn't concerned with who the men were; he was too busy counting them, one by one. Finally he reached the last one. There were twenty-six men—the exact number of "armed guards" the thwarted attacker had seen.

[Reprinted from *When Families Pray* by Cheri Fuller, courtesy of Waterbrook Multnomah Publishers, Colorado Springs, CO.]

Cheri Fuller *is a former Oklahoma "Mother of the Year" and a popular inspirational speaker. She is an award-winning author of forty-two books, including* Mother-Daughter Duet *and* The One Year Women's Friendship Devotional. *www.cherifuller.com or cheri@cherifuller.com*

More Than Coincidence

by Pamela Freeman

My husband and I sat at our dining room table filling out the forms that would decide the future of our family. For two years, we'd tried to have a child. But infertility forced us to rethink our plans. We'd prayed and prayed about what to do and every sign had led us here, to this form that would officially start the process of adopting a child from Russia. Now I felt an incredible, powerful surge of confidence that we were doing the right thing. I signed the bottom and wrote the date, March 17, 2004.

That confidence carried me through the grueling months ahead. Costs for background checks, processing fees and other requirements were high. Putting together the documents that described us, our home, our health and our finances took months of paper-chasing, visits from a social worker and repeated trips to government offices. Finally, we completed everything and waited to hear from the adoption agency.

Then the Russian government changed its international adoption laws. What should have been a few months of waiting lasted more than a year. Had we really followed God's will? I started to wonder about the sense of confidence I'd felt the day we signed the forms.

In the spring of 2006, we got a call from the adoption agency. "There's a boy in one of our orphanages in southern Russia," the person said. "We're e-mailing you the pictures."

He was a sweet little redhead, two years old. It was love at first sight. We made our travel plans. Halfway across the world, in Volgograd, Russia, my husband and I found what we'd been praying for. The boy was shy at first, but soon he was playing and cuddling with us. I held him and didn't want to let him go.

"He has some minor medical problems," the orphanage director warned, reading through the boy's file. "We don't know who his parents were. He was abandoned when he was just a few weeks old."

I looked at my husband. Did any of that matter? He was meant for us, wasn't he? The director peered down at the boy's file again.

"He was found by a police officer," she said, "on March 17, 2004."

["Mysterious Ways: More Than Coincidence" by **Pamela Freeman is** reprinted with permission from *Guideposts Books*, Copyright © 2011]

I Remember How the Fiddle Played

by Jan Fowler

I was twenty-one years old, had just graduated college, and was still filled with the wonder and fantasy of romantic idealism. For me, the world was merely an artist's canvas inviting me to splash it with a rainbow of color. Except that *my* idea of applying color was to paint with words rather than brush and easel. My passion was poetry—beautiful, inspiring, wondrous poetry. I wrote it, read it, spoke it, dreamt it.

One afternoon, while relaxing after a day of teaching at my first job in suburban Philadelphia, I was so captivated and swept away by a lyrical love poem I'd just read in *Ladies' Home Journal* that I tore it out, pressed and preserved it in my wallet, and have carried it with me ever since. The lovely poem that dazzled and bewitched me so was "Night Song" by Pegasus Buchanan.

As time moved on, I eventually fell in love, married, raised a family, and led a joyful family-centered life, but one that never allowed time for writing poetry. Decades later, however, as I approached retirement, the poet's muse whispered in my ear again and beckoned me to enroll in a poetry-writing class at a senior center in Claremont, California. I was thrilled to finally have the time to reconnect with my passion!

One afternoon during the second week of class, our instructor noted that since we only had a few remaining minutes left till the end of the hour, perhaps someone who'd brought a special poem that day might like to read it aloud right now. Eagerly, I raised my hand and was delighted to be called upon.

As I reached deep down into my purse to pull out the worn, torn, and tattered poem that I had indelibly preserved in both my memory and wallet for more than thirty years, I began. "I would like to read a lovely poem that I've deeply cherished and have carried with me ever since I was twenty-one. It's called 'Night Song' by Pegasus Buchanan."

I had barely finished my sentence when I became uncomfortably aware of a stunned silence that had fallen across the room. Embarrassed and bewildered, I couldn't imagine what on earth I had said that was wrong. Why in the world were all twenty-five students—including our teacher—suddenly staring at each other in wide-eyed confusion, then at me, then back at each other again? Eventually I heard the soft whispers "Pegasus . . . Pegasus . . . Pegasus . . ."

Mercifully, someone finally spoke. It was the teacher who managed to find her voice. "Jan, Pegasus is a member of *this class.* She's not been here because she's on a trip to Europe, but will be back next week."

Oh my gosh!" I gasped. "You mean you all *know* Pegasus? And she lives here in California?" I asked incredulously. "And are you telling me that Pegasus is a *woman*, not a man as I've always believed?"

"Yes, we know her very well," the teacher excitedly nodded. "She's been a member of our class for years and is also president of our Tumbleweed Chapter of the California Chaparral Poet's Society."

I was absolutely tingly with excitement and couldn't wait to meet Pegasus! The following week, I was awestruck when I was introduced to an unexpectedly beautiful, stately, stunning woman in her senior years. Her glowing elegance was enhanced and accented by a flowing silk scarf stylishly knotted across her classic pink sweater. So graceful, so beautiful.

She embraced me warmly and lovingly smiled. "Jan, I'm Pegasus. I'm so happy to meet and know you. Is it true you've carried my poem in your wallet all these years?" I nodded wordlessly.

"Well, I've brought you a present—my newest book of poetry," she added. Then she held up a purple bound book filled with more haunting love poems. Smiling eloquently the entire time, in it she penned the following inscription: "To Jan, who remembers how the fiddle played. Cheers and love, Pegasus."

Since then, I've read many beautiful poems written by Pegasus, but the one that always thrills and enthralls me the most is . . .

NIGHT SONG

Oh, I remember how the fiddle played,
And how we danced like wild grass in the wind,
And how the night birds joined your serenade,
And how the stars came sprinkling to rescind
The vagrant dark. And I remember love
That mingled with the laughter in your eyes,
And how the pumpkin moon hung close above
The purple hill, and how the fireflies
Fell winking through the trees and skipped among
The river reeds, and how the fish leaped up,
All silvery with night. We were so young,
I have forgotten how we filled the cup
Of youth's delight with fragile plans we made . . .
But I remember how the fiddle played!

PEGASUS BUCHANAN

Pegasus has since died, but I will always remember the thrill of our first meeting nearly twenty years ago. I remember her cherished gift book to me, which I affectionately renamed "Pegasus's Book of Passionate Purple Poetry." I remember the essence of her beauty and grace. I remember how her words danced right off the page. But most of all, I remember how the fiddle played . . .

[Poem reprinted with the kind permission of Cherie Thorgerson, copyright owner.]

Jan Fowler *is an award-winning columnist, television producer/ host, and national speaker on senior topics. She developed a passion for the senior population during her long career as a licensed speech pathologist and is now an ambassador for seniors everywhere. Jan has five grandchildren and lives in southern California. She is the founder of Starburst Inspirations, a nonprofit corporation, and is a member of National League of American Pen Women.* www.janfowler.com *or* janfowlerusa@yahoo.com

The Little Messenger

by Dora Klinova

My daughter had invited me to come visit for Thanksgiving. The guest bedroom that she and her husband had offered me happens to be the best in the house, with a large and lovely persimmon tree blooming right outside the window. By late November, these orange-yellow persimmons are so huge and ripe that they blaze like magic lanterns in sunlight!

As I sorted my belongings from my suitcase, I couldn't help but admire the scenery. The persimmon branches were so full and heavy with orange balls they looked just like Christmas decorations and lit up the room with a festive touch. Then all at once, an unexpected noise captured my attention. A little bird knocked on the window from outdoors with its beak. I was amazed.

"What do you want, little birdie?" I asked in astonishment.

The bird quickly jumped back on the branch, looked around, then leaped toward the glass again as it stretched out its wings. Suddenly, it flung its entire body against the window. Can you imagine? A small bird hitting the glass with all of its strength as though trying to enter the room! I am certain it must have been painful for the bird. Nevertheless, it hit the window at full speed again, again, and again!

If I hadn't seen this with my own eyes, I wouldn't have believed that such a small bird could perform a trick as this so purposely. I couldn't understand it and held my breath as I watched the bird cannon into the glass so strongly that the window rattled!

Finally, I sought out my children to ask about the mysterious bird.

"Oh, that's our little kamikaze," my son-in-law laughed. "The first time we heard the noise, we couldn't see where it was coming from. Then we noticed the bird and watched it with astonishment, just like you do now. This flight towards the window glass has been going on for two months."

Every morning around 6:30 a.m. when the late winter sun lightened the room, the bird began its piloting. Then it probably became tired and flew away, only to return later. This would occur at several different times throughout the day.

What did this little nestling want to tell my children? "What tidings do you bring, cute small birdie?"

Throughout this time, I should mention that my daughter was pregnant.

Why did the bird want to go through this particular window so persistently? Could it be the soul of my grandson flying joyfully as a bird? Perhaps he was announcing, "I'm coming! I'm here! Open the window! This is my room! I'm going to live here! Let me in! Let me in!"

There are many other windows in the house, but the bird only chose to hurl itself against this one particular window, which just happens to be the room where my grandson now resides.

I asked myself if my thoughts were only fantasy. Perhaps, but the repetitive, dogged ricocheting of the small bird at the hard glass was very real.

"Who were you, small wonderful nestling? Our messenger? Our guardian angel? You tried so hard to tell us something. Forgive us for not understanding. We are only human beings . . ."

Can we explain these curious events that occur in nature? They may appear as a puzzle or perhaps an inexplicable surprise, for after my little grandson, Dennis, was born, the bird amazingly disappeared.

Dora Klinova *is an award-winning writer and poet whose works have been published in newspapers and magazines and performed on stage. Her book,* A Melody from an Immigrant's Soul, *is the heartfelt story of a Russian Jewish immigrant.* dorishka2000@yahoo.com *or (619) 667-0925*

The Butterfly Riddle

by Duane Gall

It had only been a few days since my daughter-in-law, Angela, died unexpectedly from spinal meningitis at age twenty-four.

It was all so sudden. Very sad, and a great shock to us.

I had been sleeping restlessly on the living room couch instead of my bed, waking up sporadically every few hours throughout the night to write down some of my special remembrances of her. On this one particular night, I remember how I woke up, went to the dining room table, sat down, and began to write. To ease our grief, we had set up a sort of shrine in memory of Angela, so there on the same table was the wedding picture of her and my son, Soren. Next to the picture, we had also displayed Angela's nameplate from the corporation where she and I both worked.

As I sat down and began to write, from out of the corner of my eye I was distracted by what appeared to be a moth flickering down from the light. But as it fluttered and settled to land, I noticed that it was too small, too fragile, to be a typical moth. This one was a light tan, with wings that were only a centimeter each. Then a strange thought crossed my mind, "Is that a moth or is that a butterfly?" And I began to wonder what the real difference was between the two species. By now, I was fascinated because this "butterfly-moth" had perched itself on the table an inch or two above Angela's nameplate, where it just sat quietly for several seconds before slowly flying back toward the light. I glanced up to watch it circling the light, but somehow I knew it wouldn't be there. I was right. It wasn't.

Somewhat perplexed, I returned to the sofa once again to lie down. Just as I approached the couch, I suddenly noticed that there on the end table was a wooden butterfly puzzle that we had brought back from a trip to Costa Rica.

As I lay down and closed my eyes, I tried to resolve this "butterfly riddle" because I felt very strongly that Angela, herself, had somehow been present and embodied in that butterfly visitor. But if that were so, why hadn't it just landed right on *top* of her nameplate instead of a few inches above it? Doing so would have made it clear that she was present in the butterfly.

As I tried to piece it all together, I felt as if I were somehow being asked to solve this butterfly riddle. So first I considered the Costa Rica butterfly puzzle on the table next to the couch; then I reflected on my initial spontaneous question about the distinction between the butterfly and moth species.

Suddenly the answer came. I had it!

Angela's nameplate closely resembled the species nameplates that are placed below dead butterflies in museum showcases. Here was a butterfly that had been trying to convey a message to me after all. "I landed above my nameplate. I am a dead butterfly, and my species is *Angela*."

Instantly, I knew that this explanation and solution to the butterfly riddle sparkled with Angela's typical sense of humor and poetic style. And finally it came to me, and I was able to recall one final coincidence.

Angela had had a single tattoo—a small tan butterfly on her ankle.

Duane Gall *is a retired accountant who enjoys writing poetry and creating "alloy art" projects. He has been married for thirty-eight years, is the father of four, and has two granddaughters. He is also an award-winning table-tennis medalist in senior tournaments. 2619 Clermont, Denver, CO 80207 or (303)-355-8470*

Prayers in a Box

by Teresa Laudermilk

A friend of a friend who'd gone on a hiking trip to California told me about the prayer box at the top of Los Angeles's Runyon Canyon. Hikers leave a prayer or take someone else's and pray for it as they make their way along this section of the Santa Monica Mountains overlooking L.A. *Well*, I thought, *we don't have mountains like that in Oklahoma, but I love the idea!*

I talked to my pastor, who was all for it. Some members of our church crafted a prayer box and painted it white. We set it up beside a bus stop near the church. People are using it. The prayer box seems to be catching on. From a mountain trail in California to a bus stop in Oklahoma. Amen!

["Prayers in a Box" by **Teresa Laudermilk** is reprinted with permission from *Guideposts Books*, Copyright © 2011.]

Mountaintop Experience

by John E. Baker

When our church pastor invited members of our congregation to share a "mountaintop experience," an event from my early teenage years instantly came to mind. Although to many, this may not seem like such a big deal, to me it was an absolutely awe-inspiring experience that I'll never forget.

I grew up in Baltimore, Maryland, and had wanted a bicycle for many years before my dad could ever afford to buy one. As a matter of fact, I'd learned to ride well before I ever received my first and only bicycle at age thirteen. It immediately became my most prized possession.

My bike didn't arrive on Christmas Day, as planned, but one week later. I was nevertheless so excited that although the outdoor temperatures were in the frigid teens, I just had to ride it that day. So ignoring the sage advice of my mother, who insisted it was far too cold outside, I ended up being the only kid foolish enough to set foot outdoors that day. But despite the fact that my hands and ears were nearly frostbitten, it was wonderful!

I grew to love riding my bicycle everywhere, including shopping errands for my mother, and was always careful to protect it by never leaving it unattended, knowing it would never have lasted long in the government housing project where we lived.

One day, my mother asked me to ride to the A & P Grocery Store to buy a few things for her. Normally, I'd take my father's cloth shopping sack with me to hang on the handlebars later without fear of it ripping while pedaling my groceries home. But on this day, I forgot to bring his sack and could only use the brown paper bag provided by the store.

I had no sooner pedaled more than a few blocks after leaving the store when the bag ripped open! Oh, what a fine mess I was in then. I attempted to balance the torn bag full of groceries on my handlebars as I "walked" my bicycle homeward. Then, while passing a house where a woman and several children stood on the porch, the woman—who by now had noticed my predicament—kindly offered to watch over my bicycle while I made it home on foot with my groceries and could come back for it later.

But seeing all those children, I hesitated, fearing that my beloved bicycle might be destroyed by the time I returned. Noticing my hesitation, the nice lady assured me that my bicycle wouldn't be touched and that she'd guard it carefully until I came back. So I left without my bicycle, walking slowly and carefully, all the while cradling the torn bag of groceries.

But little did I know that I was far from being out of the woods yet. Just one block from home, with my house in plain view, suddenly a huge brindle-colored dog resembling a boxer appeared from out of nowhere and raced growling across the street straight towards me! At that moment, my entire body desperately cried out for immediate salvation and I heard myself scream *Oh my God* (or "Oh, something") as I braced myself for sudden death. Then, quite unexpectedly— almost as if an invisible force field had surrounded me—the dog suddenly veered and ran right on past me, barely brushing my pants leg! At that moment, I was so shaken that I dropped a bottle of vinegar and watched it shatter all over the sidewalk. (There weren't many plastic, unbreakable bottles back in those days.)

But what amazed me the most at that moment was not so much that the dog ran past me, but that my whole body felt awash in an indescribably awe-inspiring infusion of what I'll call "spirit," for lack of a better word. It was a wondrous and astonishing moment, to say the least. The sky was brighter and I had a great feeling of peace and joy. Whew!

When I returned to pick up my bicycle, I found it exactly where I'd parked it. And in spite of the broken bottle of vinegar, my mother was very proud of me for making it home under such tenuous circumstances.

Reflecting back, I now wonder what the real "mountaintop" experience was. That I found someone along my route home who could be trusted with the safekeeping of my treasured bicycle? Or that I was spared being attacked by the dog? Perhaps it was both.

John E. Baker ~ *After serving nearly twenty-nine years in the U.S. Air Force and nine years in various retail capacities, sixty-five-year-old John Baker found his calling as a church custodian, a job that he loves. Favorite hobbies include cooking, gardening, and bowling. jbaker25@ roadrunner.com*

The Forester Counselor

by Louise Lorentz

I recall an experience from the days when I was employed as a forester counselor. Such a job would never have been my first choice since I never quite pictured myself as a counselor or salesperson type. I had always been shy and quiet around people outside my own family. But fate has a way of playing tricks on us sometimes, doesn't it?

You see, my husband, John, was a forester counselor. I usually went along with him "for the ride," so to speak, because he always asked me to. Then, unfortunately, he passed away in 1965 from a heart attack. I wasn't working at the time because my job with the airbase had been transferred to Provo, Utah, and I hadn't been able to move there due to my husband's failing health. After my period of mourning following his death, the forestry district manager approached me unexpectedly one day and asked if I would take over my late husband's job.

At first, I balked like a mule!

But John had often said that should anything happen to him, he would like me to continue in his place. Considering his request, and after some additional persuasion by the manager, I thought about my situation and decided to give it a try. So in an effort to make a success of it, I studied for my license, passed the exam, and soon began working.

Those of us who were counselors always carried a projector with us to show prospective members a video about our organization, and we also lugged a large notebook that listed available plans of membership.

After experiencing a couple of disappointing weeks, I came close to deciding that this job was not for me. Then one night, I had a most vivid dream. In my dream, I was discussing my failures with my late John. And he kept telling me that I should keep on trying and that he was right there with me, just like in the days when I was right there helping *him*. It felt so real and John was so encouraging that I decided I'd reconsider and try my best to follow through with his suggestion.

So the following evening when it was time for my next appointment, I psyched myself out with positive self-talk as I walked up to the door and knocked. I was cheerfully welcomed with all my baggage. And then—*whoops!*—quite unexpectedly, I tripped on the threshold and everything I was holding scattered across their floor!

"Oh, now isn't this a fine mess!" I wailed with embarrassment. Then we all began laughing, and my clients asked if I was hurt. "No," I replied. "Just my pride." Finally, when we were all settled and relaxed I made my presentation, and ended up enjoying the evening very much.

They applied for a membership!

And after that, I continued to grow and gain confidence in my job. In fact, that particular family became some of my best friends. As it turned out, I worked for the forestry ten more years and became one of their best counselors!

I often silently thanked God for the unique way in which He blessed me.

Louise Lorentz was born prematurely, weighing only two pounds, but was determined to survive and is still going strong at eighty-five. She has worked as a big rig truck driver, day care teacher, Air Force employee, and forester counselor, and remains active in church and charity service, including reading to the blind. (909) 794-3580

Joys of a Great Grandchild

by Gerri Seaton

Everyone in the family was anxiously awaiting the arrival of my granddaughter's first baby. What joyous news! Alysia and her husband, Robert, were now nicely settled in their nearly-new house. Robert already had a thirteen-year-old son, who, along with the rest of his family, was also thrilled and excited about Alysia's pregnancy.

About that time, I had just given up driving, so had sold my car and replaced it with a golf cart. It was just perfect for transporting me around the large senior complex of eight thousand residents where I live.

Our excitement over the expected baby really surged when a large crowd of invited guests gathered with us for a festive baby shower in the park. Piles of gifts wrapped in blue—we knew it was a boy—yellow, or green were stacked everywhere for this happy event. But our dear Alysia was on her feet until late afternoon, until we finally convinced her to go home and rest after the long tiring celebration.

I wasn't at all prepared when an unexpected call came later in the day from my daughter, Debbie, saying Alysia had been taken to the hospital. The baby wasn't due yet, so by now, my heart was racing. Apparently Alysia's blood pressure had gone sky high and the baby would be coming early. I was kept informed of progress—it was a time of great tension for us all.

Baby Trent was indeed born early and weighed in at only three pounds. Without a car, I was very grateful that my daughter had offered to pick me up so she and I could drive to the hospital together to visit mother and baby. But when we arrived, we learned that only two family members were allowed in the room at any one time. Besides the shock of seeing the baby hooked up to so many tubes and machines, we learned that Alysia's blood pressure was still extremely high.

Alysia was unable to breastfeed Baby Trent, but he took to the formula quickly. He was tiny and red at birth, and born with a hernia near his navel that would require surgery later.

Now, however—almost a year later—Trent's progress is a miracle! In fact, it's hard to believe that Trent is the same baby. He's very alert, inquisitive, is gaining weight, and growing rapidly. And what a magical smile he has. His smile is so unbelievably beautiful that it makes *me* smile too!

Trent crawls everywhere, even up the stairs, so Alysia and Robert have child-proofed the entire first floor. He pulls himself up with great determination and is even trying to take steps; we predict he'll be walking by his first birthday. The doctor says he's developing normally in every respect—physically, socially, and mentally just like a full-term baby.

Trent is always the star of the show and center of attraction. Plans for his first birthday party are already underway and will be held in a big park where pony and train rides are offered. Family, friends, and many gifts will surround him. Trent may not know it is his birthday, but *we* will.

We are so proud of this little angel, a glorious and amazing gift from God!

Gerri Seaton is seventy-seven years old and has loved writing poetry and short stories since third grade. She is a member of Leisure World Creative Writer's Club, and enjoys writing words of encouragement, scriptures, and prayers to young U.S. Marine recruits going through boot camp in southern California, some of whom feel lonesome, homesick, and scared.

Chapter 2:
FALLING IN LOVE AGAIN

Five Small Diamonds

by Myrna Lou Goldbaum

I remember the time I was working at a Colorado fair when an older gentleman approached me to ask if he could please have his palm read. My poster, which read "SOUL MATE SPECIALIST," had apparently caught his eye. When we first began the reading, I could see that his first love had been twenty years old, but that it had never led to marriage. He had offered, but she'd turned him down because he was about to leave for the service. She feared he might not return home and refused to promise to wait.

His immediate response and reaction to my reading was an overwhelming "Yes!" He quickly added, "Flying in a plane over Guadalcanal, I even carried her picture in my watch fob on a chain all through the war. But when I returned home she had already married someone else."

I continued my reading. "You were married at age twenty-seven and your marriage lasted fifty years, but you've been a widower now for about a year."

Nodding, he asked, "And are you able to see the experience that I just had?"

Oh, yes. I could see that his old flame had reappeared in his life once more, and also that something very wonderful was about to happen. It was then that he began to relate his inspiring story.

As a Peoria, Illinois, native, he was an alumnus of Peoria High School and his alumni newsletter carried the announcement of his wife's death. His old girlfriend—the love of his youth who, by now, had lost her own mate four years earlier—read his name in the newsletter, then spent four months trying her best to track him down. First, she called their high school, then the Chamber of Commerce, his relatives, as well as old Illinois friends. At last, she was able to locate the brother of his best friend who explained that this gentleman was living in Colorado Springs. She called Information and finally got his telephone number.

"I see that you have been in contact," I said, adding, "and I see travel, plus a move in the near future."

"Yes, she lives in Texas!" he excitedly explained. "When she called me, I almost fell down. She said she was lonely and invited me to her home, so I immediately went to see her the very next day! We spent one wonderful week together and quickly rekindled our love.

"While we were out shopping at the mall one day, I managed to slip into a jewelry store while she was next door in a dress shop. I asked to see engagement rings, so the storeowner pulled out two trays of assorted rings to show me. Some were beautiful solitaires, while others were set with smaller diamonds.

"As soon as she came out of the dress shop, I called her into the jewelry store and proposed right there on the spot. Well, she cried, I cried, the store owner, and all the sales clerks cried too. We were so happy that they even snapped a picture of us to use in their ads. When I told her she could choose any ring at all, she pushed the solitaire ring tray aside. 'This one,' she said, and pointed and smiled. "I'd like a simple ring with five small diamonds set in platinum.'

"It was not one of the more expensive rings on display so I was perplexed, and had to ask what made her decide to select that particular ring. 'It has five diamonds,' she replied with a smile, 'which will always represent the five decades when we missed being together.'

"So now I'm moving to Texas! I plan to take care of her for the rest of our days," he said, beaming with excitement.

Myrna Lou Goldbaum *is a master palmist years with sixty years'* *experience reading forty-seven thousand palms. She is a teacher, coach,* *entertainer, TV producer-host of "Soul Mate Connections," and author* *of* May I See Your Hand?, Soul Mate Connections, *and* Diary of a Palm Reader. *(303) 651-6273.* <u>*www.myrnaloupalmistry.com*</u> *or* <u>*hmg@ privatei.com*</u>

Wedding Bells Ring Again

by Staff Writer

Sitting at what was known as the "Happy Table" in the dining room of Mission Commons retirement complex in Redlands, California, proved to be *truly* happy for two of the diners—Rose Green and David Booth, who have since become husband and wife. It was because friends who always gathered at this table seemed to have such a good time laughing, talking, and enjoying one another's company that it was so named.

Rose had been a widow for twenty-two years and David a widower for five. He would often ask Rose to please sit with him at this special table, but Rose explains that she was just too shy. However, she always noticed and liked the way in which David helped others at the complex. So one day when he offered to drive her to the local Rite Aid drugstore so she could get a flu shot, she accepted his help. And yet each time he invited her to lunch, she admits that she always "squirmed out of it."

Then David went into the hospital for a month. During that time, Rose moved to a different retirement center called The Village, also in Redlands, but she returned to Mission Commons every week so she could continue to dine with her friends.

One day, David came to The Village with some of their friends to play dominos, after which he began calling Rose and finally convinced her to have dinner with him. In March, they went on an outing at a nearby winery, plus dinner at the Olive Garden restaurant, after which the activities director at Mission Commons couldn't help noticing that the couple seemed "all googly-eyed."

David continued to visit Rose at The Village, and one day he asked to kiss her but her walker was in the way. He exclaimed, "I almost fell flat on my face!" Then in April, he proposed and gave her both an engagement and a wedding ring and one week to decide. Her answer to him was "Yes!"

Both wanted to get married immediately, but their families asked them to please wait until school was out so they could help plan the wedding. So David and Rose delayed their plans until June, at which time a Hawaiian-themed wedding was organized and held at The Village. Many of their friends from both retirement complexes joined them for the happy occasion to share in their joy.

Retired Monsignor John Ryan of a local Catholic church performed the wedding ceremony and called it the most remarkable service he had officiated at in his sixty years as a priest.

Geane Jacob, a housekeeper at Mission Commons, was wedding vocalist and performed a Hawaiian love song while Rose walked down the aisle with her seven children. David's daughter stood up with him at the wedding. It was a very happy and joyous celebration.

Rose noted that many people their age who are alone are very set in their ways, give up on the hope of ever finding the companionship of marriage again, and as a result, miss out. "Monsignor Ryan always tells people not to be afraid to live!" Rose added.

The couple now share their new life together at their retirement complex, where they continue to enjoy and celebrate their newfound love.

Great New Life after Fifty!

by Alma Visser

I'll never forget the evening when a very strange and wonderful man came into my life—Teunis Visser. Of course, I suppose he could also say the same about me—that I, *too,* am strange and wonderful. As is the case so often in life, we can never predict when or where the person of our dreams might suddenly show up. For us, it was in a hot pool, of all places, a bubbly, crowded hot pool! We were both joining in the fun of a casual Friday night party sponsored by the Jewish Singles Club in Los Angeles, not far from where each of us lived. The chemistry and attraction we felt for each other that night sparked the beginning of a long and beautiful romance. That wonderful, magical, life-changing evening was thirty years ago!

Teunis and I soon discovered that we came from vastly different backgrounds and yet found we could easily accept and respect one another's differences. Whereas I grew up in New York and had a wonderful career as an early childhood educator, Teunis was born in Rotterdam, Holland, and lived his teenage years under the oppressive Nazi occupation of his country. Following the war, he married and migrated to Canada where he earned a master's degree in chemistry and physics. Then, after becoming a Quaker, he lived in and became the manager of the Quaker Meeting House, an old mansion located in downtown Toronto.

He and I began to date frequently and Teunis soon became an integral part of our family life. Though he was widowed and I was divorced, we both appreciated and enjoyed the loving bonds of family. And when we did marry on May 5, 1985, what a glorious day it was! It so happened that I was approaching my fiftieth birthday, which was close to Mother's Day, so when asked about gifts, I said I only wanted one present. And that was to celebrate! Teunis and the Rabbi Native agreed on many issues, one of which was reincarnation. Teunis's mind has always been filled with a never-ending complexity of subjects and ideas he loves to discuss, including such things as the Hopi Indians and their plight.

And so this strange and wonderful man opened up many new adventures for me, for I'd been a single mother for fifteen years. For example, two years earlier when I was forty-eight, I recall how Teunis took me on my very first camping trip and how I loved it! Although I've always enjoyed the refreshing outdoors, sleeping in a tent was a completely new and bold experience for me. Since then, we bought a truck with a camper shell and collapsible tent and have experienced the beauty of many state and national parks on cross-country trips. We've seen the giant redwoods; we've enjoyed the pristine beach, dunes, and lagoon of Cape Canaveral National Seashore in Florida. To this day we still go camping, but now prefer closer destinations such as Agua Caliente in San Diego County where we can soak in the warmth of the natural hot springs.

Our travels have taken us to Europe many times to visit Teunis' family, and have also included Italy and the Aeolian volcanic island chain, especially Lipari, the setting of a twelfth-century novel that Teunis is writing. Now that we're both in our senior years, we cherish the deep friendship and companionship that we share, as both are meaningful and important to us. Teunis has helped ease me through several surgeries and will again be by my side as I undergo a cataract operation soon.

Our never-ending tale continues to be very joyful and eventful. Yes, I can truly say I've definitely enjoyed a great new life after fifty!

__Alma Visser__ is a seventy-five-year-old retired early childhood educator. She is also a mother, wife, grandmother of seven, and great grandmother of two. Today she is an active volunteer in literacy and preschool programs, as well as for Hadassah and temple activities. (909) 597-5407

Finding Healing and Romance at Loma Linda

by David R. Weir

My personal sojourn to Loma Linda, California, began in late January 2008, following a treacherous two-day drive over snowy mountain roads from my home in Denver. Like many other men diagnosed with early-stage prostate cancer, I had little knowledge or concern about this issue until an elevated PSA test, followed by a confirmation biopsy, captured my attention faster than one of Superman's speeding bullets.

Typical of what others may have experienced, I was offered the options of surgery, external beam radiation, and internal radiation "seeding" as viable courses of treatment, with no mention of possible nasty side effects that might impair continence or sexual potency. While pondering what, if anything, I should do about my situation, I ran across the annual "Medicine and Hospital" issue of *U. S. News and World Report* while passing through an airport during the fall of 2007. In it was a full-page ad describing the proton radiation program at Loma Linda University Medical Center, with a toll-free number to call.

Whether this ad caught my eye by coincidence or divine intervention is hard to say, but I couldn't wait to get back to Denver to check things out. In addition to receiving a timely orientation packet and video from Loma Linda, I was quickly put in touch with prostate cancer survivor Bob Marckini and his book, *You Can Beat Prostate Cancer . . . And You Don't Need Surgery to Do It.*

After reading the book and speaking with Bob on the phone, I instinctively knew that this was the best way for me to go. And so today, I count myself as one of the lucky alumni of the LLUMC proton radiation program. I was not only healed from cancer with no nasty side effects, but I also experienced the very best of Loma Linda's motto and philosophy—to "heal the whole person."

And now, as Paul Harvey was famous for saying, for the rest of the story . . .

Unlike most of the other men going through the ninety-day treatment program at Loma Linda with their wives in residence with them, I came alone as a newly minted Medicare-age single. Yes, I admit I was open to meeting other singles in the area, but had no expectation of actually doing so as golf, swimming, table tennis, serving as a volunteer pianist in the hospital lobby, plus various support group activities, were readily available.

Then everything changed in a "New York minute" when I attended a free ballroom dancing lesson, taught by Reuben Aguilar at the Loma Linda Senior Center, in early February; I met a lovely lady by the name of Jan Fowler. Jan just happened to be at this senior center in connection with a television segment she was hosting from a nearby cable station in San Bernardino; the segment was for her show, "Jan Fowler Presents: Senior Moments."

It didn't take long before Jan and I became both dancing and romantic partners—in the midst of my "radiation vacation" and beyond. Forget about winning the lottery; I had just discovered the lady of my dreams! Whether our meeting was just coincidence or, again, divine intervention I sometimes wonder, but I can say for sure that it was another life-changing event for me during my journey of healing at Loma Linda. So in more than one way, I feel I have been blessed by my whole experience.

And yes, in case you're wondering, Jan and I continue to dance together in the direction of our dreams! Carpe diem.

David R. Weir *is a sixty-eight-year-old father and grandfather. He has been an avid reader, golfer, table tennis player, swimmer, volunteer pianist, hiker, and traveler since his retirement from a long career in public health administration and related consulting work. David grew up in a small town in Nebraska and now spends most of his time in southern California.*

The Courage to Place the Ad

by Shirley A. Lamb

I was fifty-eight when my husband Glen died two months after our fortieth wedding anniversary. I was eighteen years old when I married him. Having raised nine children, I was determined not to hibernate following his death and continued to socialize as much as possible with family and friends. Several special lady friends and I saw each other often, enjoyed fun excursions together, and always with lots of laughter. And my coupled friends were thoughtful enough to include me in dinners or potluck suppers as well.

But I knew I didn't want to spend the rest of my life alone, especially after having had the closeness of a partner for forty years.

I stayed actively involved in church events, plus community theater where I acted in plays and served on the board in our southern California town of Redlands. I always enjoyed attending all family birthday gatherings and holiday celebrations, so it wasn't that I lacked a social life; I just missed having an escort whenever I attended a function alone—even a Sunday Mass, a local movie, or something as casual as Market Night.

One year, when I learned that Yellowstone National Park was hiring seniors for the summer, I even took a job there as a waitress. It was fun and though I made many new friends, I met no men. Then seven years went by. And though I'd participated in lots of community events in my hometown, I still wasn't meeting anyone whom I was attracted to and wanted to spend my time with.

Then one weekend, the "Senior-meet-Senior" listings in the *Riverside Press Enterprise* newspaper caught my eye and I began looking through these ads. Some were funny, others sounded demanding, but I certainly never saw one I'd consider answering. Yet one day when I asked my daughter, Sue, what she thought about my placing an ad, her immediate reply was, "Go for it, Mom!" I guess it was just what I needed to hear. There was no charge to place an ad, so I decided to call, expecting a computer to give me questions to answer. Instead, I got a live voice, a young man who asked what I wanted to say in my ad. Well, I became so flustered I said I'd think about it and call back.

Finally, I sat down and mustered up the courage to write an ad. When I called back, the same young man answered and cheerfully responded, "Oh, good, you called back!" At this point, I was dying inside!

So here's what I wrote: Active WWF (widowed white female), 65, interested in an LTR (long term relationship). Enjoys theater, movies, walking, gardening, some sports, travel, mountains and beach. Like to meet a fun and active gentleman, nonsmoker. (After losing my husband to lung cancer, I definitely didn't want to date a smoker).

I was given a number to call twice a week, along with a code to access responses to my ad. If I called more than twice a week, there'd be a charge. The ad came out in the Sunday paper, so I waited a few days before calling. To my surprise, there were three calls. I decided to call one back, and we met for coffee . . . But no sparks between us at all.

A few days later, however, I checked again and this time there was a response from a really nice-sounding gentleman. But when I hung up after listening to it, I started berating myself out loud, "What on earth are you doing? You're too old for this!" Afterwards, I couldn't bring myself to return his call.

One week passed, and after my daughters asked if I'd had any more responses, I decided I would check again. Yes, there were more calls, including a second one from that very same nice-sounding gentleman. This time, I was intrigued, so decided to call him. He wasn't home, so I left a message (I was careful to leave my first name only and phone number).

Well, it wasn't long before he called me back, and we chatted for forty-five minutes. I asked him to tell me about himself. Up front, he told me he was bald and I indicated that wouldn't bother me. The more we talked, the more we discovered many common interests. For example, he'd been active with the 4-H club for thirty-five years and I'd been involved with California Women for Agriculture. And whereas I'd always worried that any man would be intimidated by my family of nine children, he turned out to be the father of seven. Now that was one hurdle I could ignore (whew!).

We decided to meet for dinner the following Saturday at a Black Angus Restaurant. I told him my hair was white and I'd be wearing black so he'd know me.

Before leaving home that Saturday, I made sure my daughters knew the license number of my car, the exact time and place I was meeting him, and if they didn't hear from me by 10:00 p.m., they were to call the restaurant and have me paged. If no response, then they were to notify the police. (I'd seen enough TV shows to know there were bad people lurking out there, and I wanted a plan in place.)

As I pulled off the freeway for the restaurant that night, I began having second thoughts. So I parked in a shopping center while I sat and argued with myself, wondering if I should actually meet this man. Again and again, I asked "What on earth are you doing at this age?" Then I finally decided it would be very rude on my part not to show up, plus there was always the possibility that *he* wouldn't show. "That's it. He won't show!" I said with relief.

So I overcame my hesitation, drove across to the Black Angus, walked slowly to the entrance, and entered. Well, he did show up, being the gentleman that he is. He had been standing off to the side, saw me immediately, and introduced himself. We were seated, ordered, and talked for the next three hours, finding that we were extremely comfortable with one another. So much so that I invited him to my home for a barbecue to meet my children the following Friday!

Five months later Jim Lamb proposed, and ten months after that we were married. That was nearly ten years ago.

I'm *so* glad I had the courage to place that ad!

Shirley A. Lamb *is a seventy-six-year-old retired medical transcriptionist, mother of nine, grandmother of nine, who lives with husband Jim on "Lamb's Roost" in the foothills of Yosemite National Park, where they have a small boysenberry farm. She enjoys writing, being active in community theatre, painting rocks, and serving as president of the women's guild at her church. (559) 658-8587*

Classmates Marry
Sixty-One Years Later

by Staff Writer

Annella Barlow and Dale King had no idea when they both graduated from Redlands High School in 1948 that some sixty-one years later they would become husband and wife. Both natives of Redlands, California, the couple attended junior high school together and were also members of the youth fellowship group of First United Methodist Church. But the two never dated each other.

After graduating from high school, they each went their separate ways, married other people, and had children; Annella had three and Dale had four. Every five years, they caught up with one another at Redlands High School class reunions.

Both Dale and Annella's husband worked for the California Division of Highways (Caltrans), but Dale left the department in the 1950s. He was a civil engineer and moved from Redlands to work as city engineer and public works director for the city of Montclair some forty miles away. He also founded L. D. King Engineering Co., Inc., in nearby Ontario. Annella's husband, William Nelson Barlow, however, remained at Caltrans until he retired.

Annella, herself, enjoyed a wonderful career as a nursery school and preschool music teacher in the Redlands area, plus volunteered her time as storyteller at the Smiley Library Children's Story Hour. She was also highly recognized and applauded for leading two youth choirs at First United Methodist Church for forty-five years.

Music had always been a large part of Annella's life, and while she was preparing a Christmas program at her preschool in 1998, her husband died. She said her working with the children helped her greatly through her grief.

Dale's wife, Joy Maxine King, died in 2008. When he attended the next high school reunion he was still grieving, so the day after the event, Annella sent him the names of three women whom she thought he might want to see. But the following day he called Annella and invited *her* out instead.

It was Annella's first date since her husband's death ten years earlier. And whereas she felt admittedly "content" as she was, she nevertheless decided to accept Dale's invitation. Afterwards, she said, "We found we had such a great deal in common." It didn't take very long for them to discover how much they enjoyed being with each other.

Whereas Annella had remained involved with church, Dale had drifted away after high school. But very soon he felt motivated to begin driving the two-hour distance from his home at the beach in Carlsbad just to attend church with Annella.

Then Dale suggested that they live together and when Annella said no, she didn't do that, he proposed marriage. A wedding date was soon set for April 18, 2010, in Annella's church. She sold her house in just three weeks, and afterwards stayed in town with friends so she could complete two more programs at her preschool before moving to Dale's home in Carlsbad.

"Dale and I both feel that God had a hand in our decision to marry. It was just hard leaving my students," Annella reflected. And the director of her preschool program said Annella would be extremely difficult to replace.

Following a belated honeymoon fishing trip to Vancouver, British Columbia, the couple lives in Carlsbad, where Annella is able to continue sharing her lifelong passion for music. She has already been joyfully involved with youth by helping to teach music to seven thousand school-aged children who visit and tour the famous nearby fifty-acre Ranunculus gardens called "The Flower Fields."

Dale recently became ill with cancer and is completing a series of medical treatments. Annella said they are very grateful for the prayers of friends and church members in both Redlands and Carlsbad, as well as for the outstanding medical care he is receiving.

Annella has devoted herself to being at Dale's side throughout his treatments, cheerfully and optimistically insisting, "I consider it both a privilege and a blessing to have someone as wonderful as Dale to care for!"

Too Young to Give Up on Life

by Myrna Goldbaum

Once, while working at a University of Colorado Hospice Benefit where I read palms, there was a man whose palm I read who was particularly impressed by my reading. He was a rather distinguished-looking gentleman in his late sixties, six feet tall with sparkling blue eyes, who said he had an issue he'd like to discuss with me. It seems that eight months earlier he had been widowed, and this event was his first time out socially.

"I'm too young to give up on life," he explained.

I had told him that he had a full life, with pleasure and obligations that filled his hours. He said he was a doctor who was not yet ready to retire. And that even though he had family and friends, he said it didn't satisfy him. "I've been corresponding with a pen pal," then admitted it was a woman in Prague. "Do you have any suggestions on how we can get together?"

He then informed me that he was taking the month of December off.

"Well then, why not travel to Europe in December?" I asked him. "You could write and tell her you'll be available during a portion of the trip." What an obvious solution to this problem!

I didn't hear from him until February, at which time he phoned and left me a message. When I returned his call, I recalled his palm instantly.

"I can visualize your palm," I began. "Yours was a forty-year marriage and then your spouse died. Your second connection appears in your life in your late sixties. This new woman is your soul mate. You will correspond with one another, meet, and then spend many happy hours together," I continued. "I see her relocating to this area when you will formally date, become lovers, and then marry."

"Oh!" he breathed. "You hit the nail on the head! That's exactly what's been happening!

"She's moving here to my hometown this spring. I plan to go to Prague to help her close the sale of her home and sell her antique furniture. We will then return to Boulder together, where she's renting a home down the lane from me."

I continued my reading. "She is a few years younger than you and has been alone for ten years since the death of her husband. She's a pretty lady, intelligent, interesting to talk to, plays classical piano, and is lively. She's also a kind-hearted person who liked you immediately from the sound of your letters to her. There is no friction or any kind of manipulation between you."

"When should we plan to marry?" he asked.

"Things will fall into place when they are supposed to," I said, "and when that happens, it will be time for a frank discussion. You are in her thoughts and she is in yours. You both have a special mental telepathy that most people don't have. She is intuitive and spiritual, kind, gentle, and caring.

"And I see that you are a truly loving, generous, giving man. All of these characteristics meshed together can only make this union very magical. It's a win-win situation for both of you."

He thanked me for the advice, and I sensed that he was now at peace.

It was only later that I learned the follow-up on this couple. They did become engaged, got married, and are still married ten years later. So it must have been fate, and it worked for them.

Myrna Lou Goldbaum is a master palmist with sixty years' experience reading forty-seven thousand palms. She is a teacher, coach, entertainer and TV producer-host of "Soul Mate Connections." Myrna is also the author of May I See Your Hand?, Soul Mate Connections, *and* Diary of a Palm Reader. *(303) 651-6273* www.myrnaloupalmistry.com *or* hmg@privatei.com

The Second Time Around

by Ellie O'Brien Abshire

The voice on the other end of the phone said, "Ellie?" Thinking it was another bothersome solicitor, I curtly replied, "Yes!" "You will never guess who this is," he said. "No, who is it?" I asked rather impatiently. "Think back to 1951," he replied. Oh my goodness, I gasped silently, then heard myself reply "Oceanside, California?"

"Yes", he answered, "and I am looking at a picture of a cute little sixteen-year-old sitting on the fender of my '39 Ford with the leopard upholstery."

Right then, I immediately knew it had to be Ron, the teenage boy I had dated for three months way back in our junior year of high school!

My stepfather had been in the Marine Corps at Camp Pendleton, California, then was transferred to the East Coast, so my parents allowed me to stay and live with another Marine family just long enough to finish out my semester at Oceanside High School. It was during that short period of time that Ron and I were sweethearts. Then once I moved back east to join my family, we lost touch with each other for fifty-seven years.

Ron married young, joined the Marine Corps, and later had a career in commercial farming. He was married for fifty-two years before losing his wife to Alzheimer's Disease. I married an Air Force pilot who also retired from the military and then had a career in environmental planning. He and I were married for forty-five years before he lost his battle with cancer. After his death I started a new life with lots of community service, travel, and family togetherness, but romance and dating never even entered my mind.

Due to his wife's declining condition, in 2005 Ron had moved to a military retirement home about two hours away from Camp Pendleton because it provided care for Alzheimer's patients. It was there that a military friend mentioned the name of the Marine family with whom I had once lived in Camp Pendleton. Ron decided to contact them and he asked if they were still in contact with Ellie, the young girl who'd lived with them those many years ago—me!

"Yes," came the reply, "and she lives only twenty minutes from you."

By now, Ron's wife has died, so he finally tracked me down in Redlands, California, and called me. We talked and talked and then he and I met again on September 12, 2008. Something magical happened. We immediately felt a connection!

Six weeks later we announced our engagement to our families and friends. Although we had once been "married" by "Marryin' Sam" at the Sadie Hawkins Dance in high school, we were married for real on December 27, 2008, with all thirty of our immediate families present. Amazingly, this second romance took place over three short months, the same period of time we had dated in high school!

We can't explain our feelings except to say that we both had wonderful spouses and wonderful lives. And now, we have started a new phase, a tremendous adventure, where "Love is wonderful and easier the second time around."

We thank God every day for our special blessing!

Ellie O'Brien Abshire and husband, Ron, live in Redlands, California. Ron is a retired USMC officer, has nine grandchildren, loves golfing, collecting stamps, and traveling. Ellie is a former University of Redlands employee who plays tennis, volunteers in her community, enjoys her eight grandchildren, and stays in touch with many of her former foreign exchange students from Chile, Colombia, Sri Lanka, Japan, Mexico, and China. (909) 793-6032

Chance Meeting

by Judith Tischler Rogers

There he was, dashing down the hall, scarf flying behind him, looking very debonair. And I immediately thought, "Now *there's* someone I'd love to meet when it's time to choose dinner partners!" Soltero, a newly-formed singles group in Colorado Springs, was holding their first social mixer that evening.

Since I happened to be one of the six advisory board members, I was invited to help plan and structure Soltero events. Our promoter was the membership director of the Plaza Club, a premier eating club. I had recently moved to the Springs to accept the position of vice-president of development and community relations at a major hospital in June of 1986 and often took potential donors to lunch at the Plaza Club, which is how I came to know its membership director.

I was fifty years old, had been divorced for ten years, and found it easier to make women friends more quickly than men. Now, only four months since my move, I decided that as the newest resident on the advisory council, I would volunteer to be the woman greeter at the entrance to the Plaza Club. After all, what better way to get an early overview of the guests?

Our advisory group had set some parameters for this first event. First, we limited it to fifty men and fifty women, all of whom either had to be a member of the Plaza Club itself or be invited by a Plaza Club member. We decided that dinner partners would be matched by choosing matching playing cards. Seat assignments for a Nell Carter concert—which was scheduled between dinner and dessert—would be determined by having each guest pick a ticket; odd-numbered seats for men and even for women.

Once my co-greeter, Ray, and I had carefully explained the procedure to the group, he and I began the process of locating our own dinner partners. Of course, I went directly over to the man who had worn the scarf and asked, "By any chance does my card match yours?" He smiled at me warmly and answered, "No, but I sure wish it did!" I replied, "Thank you."

We both moved on and I can't even recall who my dinner partner was. Then came the announcement that it was time for us all to walk over to Symphony Hall. And suddenly, there he was—the man with the scarf—standing right at my side by the dinner table. He introduced himself as Jim and asked if he could please walk me to the performance.

Every detail of that evening is still clearly etched in my mind. We weren't seated next to each other at the performance or even in the same row. However, after our two-block walk to the concert together, he had asked if he could also escort me back later and join me for dessert. Although the Nell Carter performance was beautiful, I am sure my mind was distracted and kept wandering to possibilities about my new acquaintance, Jim.

We shared our walk back to the Plaza Club with an attractive younger woman who had sat next to Jim earlier and who was intent on making advances toward him. She nestled up against him on the elevator as we rode up to the top floor. I tried to stifle my jealousy. But once we'd all arrived and hung up our coats, Jim took my hand, smiled, and said, "Let's find a table for two where we can talk."

We thoroughly enjoyed eating dessert together, then fell right into the swing of things by rhythmically dancing to both slow and fast numbers played by a wonderful, upbeat four-piece combo. Not only did I discover that Jim was a beautiful dancer, but he surprised me by singing softly in my ear with his pitch-perfect voice. I felt like the costar in a Technicolor movie!

When the party ended at 11:30 p.m., Jim walked me to my car and asked me to have dinner with him the following Wednesday night at my favorite restaurant. Twenty-four years later, we still continue our delightful adventure together as "married sweethearts!"

Judith Tischler Rogers *is a seventy-four-year-old wife, mother, stepmother, and grandmother who enjoyed a twenty-two-year career as a fundraiser that began at the University of Pennsylvania. She is a retired teacher with a love of music, travel, history, the outdoors, and church volunteer work.*

New Love after Cancer

by Fred Belk

Fifty-four years after Virginia and I had both attended the same small college in Missouri, she and I were married. Years ago, although we had known about each other through mutual friends, including a roommate, we can't ever recall speaking directly to one another.

Virginia's roommate and one of my closest buddies were students in the same history department where I was also a major. Virginia, however, was majoring in elementary education. In those days, both she and I worked almost full-time to pay expenses, so neither of us had much time for dating. Then two years later, she married my buddy. He died eight years afterwards, however, of complications from childhood diabetes.

It was only at our thirty-year college reunion that Virginia and I finally spoke and had the chance to meet each other. It was then that I learned about my friend's death, which had occurred some twenty years earlier. By now, Virginia had already remarried and I was introduced to her second husband at the reunion. She and I struck up a conversation in which I shared news of my recent unhappy divorce, and we also discovered that I had once worked only thirty miles or so from where she lived and taught in Navajo land.

As it turned out, I was planning to move to New Mexico, so we agreed to exchange Christmas cards and perhaps get together for a meal and friendly chat because, by southwestern standards, our homes were not prohibitively distant. Although we did exchange greetings sporadically, we never actually saw each other in person.

Then as time moved on, I developed prostate cancer and underwent proton therapy at Loma Linda University Medical Center in California. Afterwards, I wrote Virginia to ask for the latest contact information on some of our mutual friends, as well as for the latest update on her life. But no word until six months later. Then, upon returning home to New Mexico from my six-month medical checkup in California, I found her response waiting for me.

After nearly thirty-four years, Virginia was widowed *again!*

I called her and that's when we really began comparing notes. She was active in the same church denomination as I. We discovered that we each liked the color blue, oysters, angel food cake, music, and art. Virginia has a trace of Choctaw blood, and one of my dearest friends was a Choctaw Indian. She attended second grade in California, and I had been conceived there. The list went on and on . . .

Two hours later, we decided to continue our conversation in person, and we've been talking ever since!

She and I have been married nearly two years now and have amalgamated our households and lives slowly and judiciously. Although we need and appreciate those senior discounts and perks, it's our love that makes us young at heart. Virginia and I look forward to sharing many more years of retirement activities, plus pursuing many of our passions, which are based on mutual beliefs and philosophies. It's wonderful and fulfilling to find new love after cancer!

Fred Belk is seventy-three years old and still actively engaged in some of his former pursuits as a social worker, minister, college professor, art dealer, and writer. P.O. Box 1941, Tijeras, NM 87059

Love Lasted Sixty Years

by Staff Writer

June 14, 2010, was a special day in the lives of Russell Light and Patsy Prince. It was the day they exchanged wedding vows some sixty years after they had parted in Ohio, where they had been high school sweethearts.

"I love her and I have for sixty years!" he proclaimed happily as they exchanged vows in his hospital room shortly before he was to undergo an angioplasty heart procedure. For her part, Patsy said she couldn't believe that someone could possibly care for and remember her for that many years.

Patsy and Russell had dated when she was only sixteen and he eighteen. He then joined the army, served during the Korean War, and on a return trip home in 1951 intended to marry her, but found out that by then she had changed her mind. Russell continued to serve in the army, both as a paratrooper and commander in a rifle company in Korea before returning home permanently.

Patsy was married in 1952, but later divorced and remarried. Thirty years ago, she and her new husband moved to Redlands, California. Two years afterwards, however, the couple returned to Ohio where her husband died of brain and lung cancer. She then came back to Redlands to live.

Russell also got married in 1952. He left the army to attend college in Athens, Ohio, then taught school and was a coach in Cincinnati for thirty-five years. In 1977, he retired as a major, having served in the National Guard and Reserves. But in 2009, his wife died, also from lung cancer.

It was then that he began searching for Patsy.

Patsy was taken by great surprise when she received an e-mail saying that Russell was looking for her; yes, she recalled her former boyfriend. Normally, she is very cautious about opening unknown e-mails but this one captured her attention. "He used my maiden name," she explained. Soon they were talking by phone—three hours the first time—and then he began sending her flowers at her worksite every week. They scheduled a dinner date for March, when she had a trip planned back to Ohio to visit her daughter.

When they finally met each other again, although neither looked the same, Patsy smiled as she said, "His eyes had sweetness and kindness in them."

Russell then bought Patsy a cell phone, and one night after she had returned to her home in California, he called her and proposed. A week later, a package arrived at her workplace, it contained both an engagement and wedding ring.

Russell came to California soon afterwards and they set a wedding date for July 11, 2010. Soon after, however, he became ill and it was then that they learned he would need a heart procedure. So they decided to get married before the procedure and, with the hasty help of Patsy's coworkers—who quickly shopped for cake and sparkling apple cider—plus a minister whom they found online, they were able to hold the ceremony right there in the hospital. Patty was dressed in her business clothes and Russell wore a Hawaiian shirt buttoned over his hospital gown.

The Lights said their families were happy and supportive of their union. She has three daughters, and he has two sons and two daughters. "Between us we have twelve great grandchildren," Patsy said.

Russell was reported to be "euphoric," and Patsy said she decided she'd been alone so long because she was waiting for *him*.

One month later, the couple repeated their vows and remarried in a church ceremony on July 11, 2010. "After thirty years as a widow, of course it's different," Patsy said. "You have someone to take care of again! It's enjoyable because he's a good person. I feel very blessed."

Chapter 3:
ANIMAL BLESSINGS

Animals I Have Known

by Bobbie F. Henry

Ever since I was a young child, I've been blessed with the gift of receiving special favors from animals, many of whom have provided loving laughter and amusement for me and others who witnessed their endearing personalities, special characteristics, or entertaining antics. Over the years, friends and neighbors frequently brought injured creatures to me for treatment and care.

I recall how I once "doctored" a great horned owl who had injured his beak after flying into an auto windshield. I taped his beak and placed him in a large cage while it healed. During that time, I set mousetraps in vacant fields to catch mice for his food, supplementing with bits of beef when the traps provided no yield. When his beak was fully healed, the day finally came for me to take him out to the field and release him into the air. Each time I tossed him up, however, he'd just circle round and round and come right back to me. But after three days of such efforts, success finally came and he did fly away.

One week later, this magnificent bird blessed me again by returning to our field and landing near my feet. As I bent down to greet him, I noticed another owl perched on a fence post nearby; then a few moments later, both birds flew away together. It was then that I realized that my fully healed "patient" had returned to show me his mate and to extend his gratitude!

Another experience involved one of the most clever pet birds we ever raised—the children's bantam rooster, whom they taught to play the piano. By placing a kernel of dried corn on specific keys, he played a tune as he ate them up in sequence. Whenever the school bus arrived and delivered the children home from school, he'd immediately follow them inside the house and "play the piano" by picking up the corn that they placed on the keys. After the last kernel, and the last piano note, he was more than happy to return to the yard.

I recall another memorable event that occurred shortly after we began life as ranchers on ten acres of farmland in Ramona, California. Soon afterwards, my husband was hired by a local automobile agency and wore their blue pants and shirt uniform to work. Coming home after his first day at work, he walked out to the pasture to greet Suzie, our milk cow, as was his habit every evening. But this time, Suzie wouldn't allow him to come anywhere near her, nor would she enter her stall to be milked, shying away each time he tried. I am proud to say I solved the dilemma following an "ah-ha" moment. Of course, Suzie didn't recognize him in a dark shirt; he always wore white shirts at milking time. So in her view, he was the definitely not the designated "milk man"! After he'd changed his blue shirt for a white one, Suzie more than willingly entered her stall and calmly provided our milk for the day.

Knowing about my special kinship and love of animals, a friend once gave me a spider monkey whom I named "Mike." He was a bright, ever-willing companion, and easily "potty trained" to use newspapers on the floor of the utility room. Mike was diligent "when nature called" while outdoors playing with the children, for he'd stop, quickly run through the front door to his paper potty, and then back outside again to play. He also loved malted milk balls, but only licked off the chocolate covering, replacing the malt ball into the dish.

Mike loved to ride to town with me and generally stood on my lap while I drove. From this position, I could safely see past him to the road. One day, however, we were the cause of a near-accident when a truck driver who was passing us only saw Mike at the wheel and not me. The thought of seeing a monkey driving a car caused him to swerve right off the road, but luckily he was able to stop safely.

Whenever the whole family was away, we locked Mike into his 6' x 8' wire cage with plenty of food, water, and a tire swing; we knew he was safe there. But one day, we were so saddened to come home and find that the lock had been broken, and Mike was gone! We only hope that whoever stole Mike treated him well and never let him stand on his lap while driving a car.

Bobbie F. Henry *is an eighty-three-old widow with eight children and thirty-seven great grandchildren who has served as a caregiver for cancer patients. She is a lifelong lover of animals and has had fifty-two pets. Bobbie's middle name is Faith and she insists she has lots of it, adding that her life "has truly been blessed." (909) 948-9018*

Just Daisy

by Sandi Appleby

By 6:15 a.m., our Chevy El Camino was loaded with many of our once-upon-a-time treasures. It was brisk but sunny for such an early morning in Florida.

When my husband, Red, and I arrived at the Community Center, our destination, we could already see the many "early birds" busily scouring the indoor and outdoor tables, eagerly scooping up items that they nostalgically remembered from their childhood era. Included in their "must-haves" were bits and pieces of assorted scrap for craft projects, as well as some genuine antiques with enough authenticity for internet resale.

We quickly got to work unpacking our own wares to sell. First, we laid out our vintage costume jewelry, then fifteen boxes of brand new outdoor lights recently purchased at a local auction specifically for this event, as well as an assortment of auto parts. By noon, when it became painfully clear that we had barely taken in thirty dollars toward the sixty we were charged for the use of our two tables, my husband and I turned to each other. "Why are we here?" we asked. But we already knew the answer.

At our summer home on the New Jersey shore, Red and I run a halfway house for rescued feral cats and kittens. We see to it that many get neutered or spayed before being released to good homes, whereas others—especially the kittens—may linger on with us for a while. We not only absorb the state-funded clinic fees of forty-six dollars per cat, but also the added expenses of food and litter once the animals return to our halfway house following their surgical procedures.

Just then, I recognized the pleasant middle-aged lady seated at the table next to us as the Community Center employee who'd arranged for us to be assigned to such a choice location inside this building. Since our love of animals also extends to dogs, I casually asked the name of her sweet and friendly pearl-gray female, which appeared to be part poodle and part schnauzer.

Once we had introduced ourselves, we struck up a conversation. Cynthia, the dog's present owner, explained that she'd actually had Daisy for only three weeks. It seems that earlier in the month, the center had sponsored an adopt-a-pet day; although Cynthia had absolutely no intention of bringing home a pet that day, there was this sweet-natured medium-size dog with hopeful eyes who sat up to paw her skirt. That did it; Cynthia just couldn't resist and brought Daisy home. She was told that Daisy's owner was a man who had died and that his family couldn't keep the dog.

Later, while searching through the yellow pages for a dog groomer, an ad for a grooming service located ten miles away caught her eye, so she called for an appointment and took Daisy in.

Much to her surprise, as soon as Daisy had entered the salon, she was met with unexpected exclamations of joy from the staff! "Daisy, where have you been?" they all shouted.

When Cynthia told them the story of the recent adoption, a staff member then told her the *true* story. Daisy's owner was a woman, not a man, who had passed away. And the reason Daisy had chosen Cynthia was because she looked just like her former owner!

Well, Red and I packed up our belongings at the end of that afternoon, dropped off some remaining items to the Cat Thrift Shop, delivered a lampshade, took home our thirty-five dollar profit, and the most wonderful uplifting story, which we'll never forget!

Sandra Appleby *is a seventy-three-year-old wife, grandmother, realtor, and retail business owner. She enjoys photography, dancing, and boating, and is actively involved in cat rescue in New Jersey. (609) 709-2956 June to August and (941) 485-5836 late September to May.*

The Summer of No Flowers

by Julie Ulmer Mathews

All summer long, we were awakened in the early dawn by the clanking of chains being dragged across our rooftop. This would not be so unusual if it were caused by a cat. But it wasn't a cat at all. It was a monkey. And the city ordinance in our southern California town doesn't allow monkeys to run free. But this was Sally, a special monkey who'd escaped from the local YMCA Youth Circus, and who was determined to avoid capture.

I was hoping that someone would catch her, or at least take the clanging metal collar off her neck so I could finish out my summer vacation by sleeping in. After all, it was the last summer before my senior year in high school and sleep was important to a teenager.

A day or two after Sally arrived in our neighborhood, Mother went outside to water the flowers that she'd planted in the spring. While tenderly cultivating those seedlings, Mom had envisioned beautiful bouquets brightening all the rooms in our house. Flowers were important to her, as she believed a bouquet of flowers brought spiritual energy into the home. Mom was now anxious to see if some were getting ready to bloom.

"Oh no," she wailed as she came running back into the house. "The buds that were beginning to open are all gone!" Mom hurried next door and asked Mrs. Dana, "What could have happened to my buds?" "I have no idea, my dear. But if you need flowers, I have some in my garden," Mrs. Dana generously replied.

Soon, they both went out to pick Mrs. Dana's flowers. Then, as they turned the corner to face her flower bed, Mrs. Dana suddenly exclaimed, "Egads!" Both stood there, staring at empty stems with no flowers or buds on the ends of those plants either. But soon Mother and Mrs. Dana felt slightly relieved when they realized that though they had no flowers now, of course more would grow and bloom to provide table bouquets.

But "soon" never came . . . Bouquets never did grace the tables in our neighborhood that fateful summer of '54. In fact, the entire assortment of flower buds on our section of West Crescent Avenue had completely disappeared. And perched up on the fence in our yard we could easily see the reason why. There was Sally, the monkey, eating away at not just one or two of the flower buds that Mother had lovingly cultivated, but gobbling up all that were available. I recall how discouraged Mother felt. All of her earlier efforts to bring flowers to the table now seemed totally in vain.

All through the summer, as Sally swung through our trees, ate our flowers, and woke us up too early in the morning, we devised imaginative schemes to catch her.

One plan was to feed her. So we gave her watermelon, plus other food, in hopes that she would get her fill and not eat our flowers. She liked the watermelon all right, and seemed to enjoy eating it while sitting atop the fence. Dad even snapped a picture of her enjoying that meal. When she was finished eating, we expected her to go swing in the trees, but she did not. No, apparently she had other ideas and wanted dessert, so she headed straight for the fresh flower buds. We were all exasperated and needed another plan.

The new plan was to not feed Sally at all in hopes she'd be forced to return to Mr. Lenker, her former owner, whose home was not so far away. But she did not. Just one more plan that didn't work.

The summer wore on as we all watched helplessly while the monkey destroyed one group of flowers and plants after another. Oh, how we racked our brains trying to devise a solution! Mr. Lenker stayed in touch with us and suggested more strategies to help catch her. But Sally was great at eluding them.

I was growing tired of trying to solve the monkey problem and began planning for my senior year at high school. One hot day in late August, as I looked through the newspaper ads for new school clothes, I saw many lovely outfits that I was dying to have. My folks would provide me with one dress and one pair of shoes, but I wanted more. Now how could I get enough money to buy all I wanted?

Just then, Mother interrupted my clothing daydreams.

Here's the glass jar Mr. Lenker suggested," she said, holding up an empty mayonnaise jar in her right hand and a green onion in her left. "When this green onion is in it, we'll have the trap to capture Sally."

I followed her outside as she opened the door to Dad's workroom. The jar with the onion in it was sitting on the workbench. "I'm going in the house to take my nap now," Mom said. "If Sally goes in and grabs the onion, just sneak up behind so she doesn't see you and close the door."

"Okay," I agreed doubtfully.

I went back inside to the dining room table where my newspaper ads for back-to-school clothes were still spread out, and occasionally glanced through the window for Sally. Sure enough, after sixteen minutes I heard her chain dragging! Sally had come around the side of our house and entered Dad's little room. I sneaked out the door so she couldn't see me and carefully tiptoed close enough to get a good look.

There was Sally with her hand inside the mayonnaise jar, clutching the onion. But as she tried to withdraw the onion, her fist got stuck inside the rim of the jar. She tugged. She pulled. She knocked the jar on the countertop but her hand would not come out with the onion in it. And Sally would not release her grasp. She wanted that onion and was determined to get it out.

As she pondered and deliberated her situation I quietly moved toward the workroom. To my surprise Sally never looked up. I reached for the door, grabbed the handle, and before she knew it, slam! Sally was trapped.

"I caught Sally, the monkey, I caught Sally, the monkey!" I yelled triumphantly as I ran in the house, waking up Mom. I was elated.

I felt like a hero. I had done what no one else had done all summer. With Mom's help of course.

"Redlands High Senior Catches Monkey!" the newspaper headline read the next day. My self-esteem soared higher and higher. It was worth something, at least the five dollar reward money. And I knew just how I'd spend it. On a brand new outfit for school, of course!

Then as I went looking through the dress shops, it finally hit me, and I began to realize that it was really Mother who'd laid the trap for Sally. Am I being selfish? *"Change your plans, girl!"* I admonished myself.

So that evening, instead of buying a new school outfit, I watched Mother's face beam with joy as I surprised her with a beautiful bouquet of assorted flowers to brighten her dinner table. I was happy, too, from the happiness of pleasing someone else.

Besides, my reward came in a different way. I'd be able to sleep in the next morning. Sally was gone. Yes, happily reunited with Mr. Lenker!

Julie Ulmer Mathews is a retired preschool teacher who has also been a recreation leader, dance teacher, and arts and crafts facilitator. Although she would like to get back to painting, she finds she's too busy writing short stories about her family, feeding the homeless, and singing at nursing homes instead.

Royal Pooch on the Loose

by Susan Snowden

"Penny's gone! She must've wriggled out through the air vent in our basement!"

The call came the day after my husband and I arrived in Connecticut for a week-long visit with his mother. It was Linda, my friend back in Atlanta, the person we'd entrusted with our precious Vizsla.

Vizslas are Hungarian pointers, the favored dog of Hungarian nobility before World War II. In her five years with us, Penny had proved that she remembered her royal heritage. She wouldn't dream of sitting on a floor unless there was an Aubusson rug on it. For snacks she preferred hearts of palm over chew sticks. And she wanted nothing to do with kennels. Whenever we tried to board her, she escaped before we pulled away.

"We've combed the neighborhood, but no one's spotted her," Linda said, frantic.

I imagined Penny roaming the streets of Atlanta, or worse, lying dead beside the road. "We'll fly back today," I said, "but please keep looking!"

My mother-in-law was crushed. She'd bought our plane tickets, not a cheap treat for a widow on a pension. But she understood that we had no choice. Our phone number was on Penny's collar, but we'd turned off the answering machine. If someone found her, they wouldn't be able to reach us. And if they took her to the pound . . . it was too horrible to consider.

The flight back to Atlanta was miserable. A thunderstorm rocked the plane, and I pictured Penny drenched and shivering in some alley. What's worse, the couple seated across from us on the plane were obviously not animal lovers; they said we were nuts to cancel our vacation because of a dog.

Back home, I broke down at the sight of Penny's water bowl. The house was dark and silent, and there was absolutely nothing we could do . . . but wait. My husband scanned the "Pets Found" ads and I stared out the window.

We'd been home almost twenty-four hours when a woman called. "Is this 352-2822?" she asked.

"Yes," I said, holding my breath. "Do you have our dog?'

"She's right here. She's fine."

When she learned of our ordeal, she insisted on bringing Penny to us right away. We were standing in the front yard as a sleek silver Mercedes pulled up, Penny riding proudly in the back seat as if being chauffeured to high tea with the Queen.

After happy tears and hugs for Penny, and lots of licks back from her, we invited our heroine inside. She told us that Penny had spent the last few days sleeping in a velvet wing chair; she'd dined on sirloin steak, and had endeared herself to everyone in the family.

"Penny had to cross an eight-lane highway and travel ten miles to get to your house," I said when I heard where they lived.

"Well, it's a good thing you flew back. We had decided that if I called today and still got no answer, we were just going to keep her!"

Susan Snowden, *an Atlanta native, now lives in the beautiful Blue Ridge Mountains of western NC. She is an award-winning poet and author, and she has worked as a freelance book editor since 1985. SnowdenEditorial.com*

The Riot Horse

by Dr. Donald E. Bidlack

Whenever people hear that I'm a retired veterinarian, they often ask, "Where was your hospital?" When I tell them I was a large animal veterinarian, they generally say, "You mean horses and cows get sick too?" "Yes," I tell them, "veterinarians can do other things besides give puppy shots." And even though most large animal calls are routine, every once in awhile one remains memorable.

Back in the 1960s, I was called to a farm to examine and treat an injured horse. The animal was a nice-looking saddle horse, but one that obviously had enough hot blood to make me extremely cautious handling it.

The owner was an experienced horseman, but there'd been an accident. He'd been leading the horse into its stall inside the barn, when suddenly the horse had reared up, striking its head on the hardwood lintel above the doorway. The laceration that now ran from ear to ear on the horse would require sutures. First, I injected a local anesthetic, cleaned the wound, trimmed its roughened margins, then closed it with several sutures. The horse didn't fight me, and the owner returned the animal to its stall.

I planned to return to inspect the wound the next week, and if it were in good enough shape, to remove the sutures. My wife, Lois, and I happened to have out-of-town visitors that week—my cousin Barbara and her husband, Ray. Ray was a police officer in Lansing, Michigan, which, like many cities in that decade, was seeing riots. Ray had, in fact, just completed advanced training in riot control, using all kinds of armor, helmets, and non-lethal weapons. I took Ray along with me on my horse call.

The owner led the horse out of its stall onto a nice grassy paddock. The horse took one look at me, then suddenly went berserk. I couldn't approach it without its trying to get me with its front or back feet or its teeth. Horses, like camels, are great biters. Despite the thrashing hooves and gnashing teeth, I administered an intravenous tranquilizer. No effect. The thrashing continued. I administered more tranquilizer, and still nothing. Someone behind me said, "If he could"—meaning the horse—"he'd start World War III, Doctor." I went to my truck, got my ropes, and arranged them on the horse. When bystanders pulled on them, what I'd hoped for did happen. The horse sat down on its rump and rolled over on its side. I was then able to straddle the horse's neck. The wound appeared to be very well healed, and I was able to successfully remove the sutures. I took my ropes back and the horse got up and went quietly with its owner to its stall.

Ray and I got in the truck. As he was hooking his seat belt, he looked up at me and suddenly blurted out, "You get killed the way you want to, Doctor, and I'll get killed the way I want to!" Horses can be as scary as riots, we agreed, and we've been laughing about that horse call of ours ever since.

Donald E. Bidlack, **DVM**, *established a large animal veterinary practice in central Indiana. He retired with a position of associate veterinary pathologist. Dr. Bidlack's writing history began with his writing technical medical research reports, but now in his retirement, he finds great enjoyment in writing for pleasure. dl-bidlk@sierratel.com or (559) 683-2706*

He Made Me Love Him

by Amber Costa

"He made me love him, I didn't want to do it . . ." Buddy was foisted on us.

My husband, Nick, and I had finally reached the nirvana of the retired. Our kids were successfully launched and our last beloved pet had just gone home to pet heaven. Yippee, we were finally free! Which is exactly when our son-in-law, Jamie, began desperately seeking a home for this "needy-with-issues," ill-tempered, grieving, five-pound cockapoo. If Buddy were taken to an animal shelter, he might be put down or adopted by folks who'd probably return him before day's end. For us, the timing couldn't have been worse. And yet, we begrudgingly gave in, knowing what we knew—we were Buddy's last chance.

Nick, who grew up with German shepherds and retrievers, said he'd be embarrassed to take this odd, rabbit-sized fluff for a walk except under the cover of darkness. Buddy was too tiny to be a "real" dog. First of all, he had an under bite and tended to curve his body into a silly-shaped *C*. Secondly, his hind legs were misaligned with his front legs, and lastly, he walked with a rightward leaning, while his left back leg skipped every few steps.

Buddy had been the empty-nest replacement for Jamie's mom, Val. He was a palm-sized puppy whom she had brought home shortly after her children left for college. The pup imprinted on her as his human mom, loving her truly, madly, deeply, and living for the moment when she would arrive home from work each day. He made her family his "pack." But that was it. His devotion and affection were for them and them only. And please, keep children and other animals far, far away; he simply couldn't abide them.

Whenever we visited Val, Buddy would bark at the door, alerting her of interlopers to be sent away. When friends and family trespassed anyway, he stayed at Val's side, waiting for them to be banished from his territory. We loved Val dearly, but considered Buddy to be yappy, standoffish, needy, and cranky.

Buddy seemed to know about Val's kidney cancer as soon as she was diagnosed. Even though he was only three years old, his chocolate coat suddenly turned gray. Over the next few years, as illness gradually took its toll on Val, a stress-induced bald patch grew from a speck in Bud's coat to a sizeable hole. He remained at Val's side when she passed away and suffered enormous grief.

So when Buddy was first brought to us, his head and tail hung low, he refused to eat and turned up his nose at any attempt of affection. His tiny mouth spewed a powerful doggy breath, probably due to sour-stomach from stress, which one would expect from the jaws of a Great Dane. And he remained glued to the doggie bed brought from his former home. I immediately took him to the vet for a dental cleaning to help freshen his breath and to update the shots I was certain he had missed while Val was so ill. But it was too much activity all at once for such a fragile creature. Buddy staggered and dropped to the ground as soon as I brought him home.

With guilty tears streaming down my cheeks, I picked him up gently while his sorrowful black eyes tenderly looked directly into mine. Just at that moment, the old song "You Made Me Love You" came on the radio, and so I began singing while rocking my head from side to side to the familiar refrain, "I didn't want to do it, I didn't want to do it." Then, lo and behold, Buddy began to rock *his* head exactly in time with mine. Love happened just like that!

Buddy soon became my Napoleonic body guard, ready to sacrifice life and limb for me. Once, in an effort to defend me, he even tried to attack a boxer, who sent him looping backwards. Throughout the next ten years, Buddy followed me from room to room or patiently waited by whichever door I'd left the house. He'd sleep on the bathroom rug while I spent an hour reading in the tub, and loved lap time in the evenings while I read the newspaper. But his favorite part of the day was bedtime, which he approached with the same joy as Peanut's Snoopy singing the suppertime song as he'd take a joyful flying leap across the room into his doggie bed.

Christmas was especially trying for Buddy, with the house so full of noisy grandchildren, scattered toys, new presents, and the racket of gift wrap being ripped and tossed about. He learned to retreat under the Christmas tree, curled up in a tiny tight ball. Buddy was persnickety, though harmless, with children, but was perfect in other ways. A huge dog could never have been more loyal.

Our much-loved and faithful fifteen-year-old Buddy died last year. I'll always remember him curled under the Christmas tree; he was our special gift. I'd like to believe that the day he died in my arms, his spirit soared to his beloved Val.

So now we've rescued Big Beulah, a hundred-pound eight-year-old golden retriever. Her former owners gave her up because she was lame. Big Beulah owes her second chance at life to tiny Buddy because his loss made our house way too empty. So now we're back to vacuuming dog hair from the carpet and finding pet care when we travel. Nick and I will probably never achieve bliss as free-wheeling retirees. But because of Buddy's legacy of love, we will keep sharing our golden years with our loveable, loving four-legged friends.

__Amber Costa__ is a retired social worker and adult school teacher. She and her husband, Nick, began their retirement by training for and completing four marathons. Both devote their time as community volunteers, serving wherever needed when not traveling or visiting with grandchildren.

To Err is Human, to Forgive is Feline

(Strive to be Feline)

by Bernie S. Siegel, M.D.

I am continually amazed at our pets' capacities for forgiveness. I constantly complain and remind my wife about the terrible things she does, such as leaving the bathroom lights on. She reminds me that I eat too fast. Meanwhile, our cats forgive us both for these and all our other horrible flaws.

If I step on one of our cat's tails, she doesn't attack me. She doesn't remind me how many times I've done the same stupid thing. She doesn't ask, "Why can't you watch where you're going?" or yell, "Watch out. Here he comes again." The cats don't like it when I brush their teeth and comb knots out of their fur, but later that night they will sit on my lap as I watch television and rest on my chest when I go to bed, purring loudly to let me to let me know they love me despite what I've done to them.

Why are they so forgiving and easy to live with, while people are so difficult? I think it is because they are born knowing something we have to discover. They know who they are and why they are here. Do you know why life was bestowed upon you? When you answer that question correctly, your life will change and you will become more loving, accepting and forgiving of yourself and others.

I look across the room at my feline teachers and I am grateful for their teachings and love. They remind me to ask the right questions. I know what I am here to do. Now I have to go and practice my purring, get my back scratched and my tummy rubbed.

I prescribed forgiveness earlier, but this is so important that I'm giving you a refill. Take a few minutes to think about forgiveness. Is there anything anyone has done that you cannot forgive? If you find yourself unable to forgive someone, go back and ask the key questions again: Why are you here? What do you need to understand? Why was life bestowed upon you? When you find the right answers to those questions, you will be almost feline in your capacity to forgive. Now you have two role models, a cat and an earthworm (more about that later). Things are looking up.

Reprinted with the kind permission of **Bernard S. Siegel, M.D.**, author of *Prescriptions for Living,* and HarperCollins Publishers.

Dr. Bernie Siegel is *a retired pediatric and general surgeon who has authored many books about the mind-body relationship between the patient and the healing process. He is a popular speaker who addresses the profound effects of peace and love upon health and wholeness. His newest book is* A Book of Miracles.

WHAT WAS I THINKING?!!

by Jan O'Leary

When the time came for us to release our ancient cocker spaniel to his final resting place, I remember how I declared, "No more animals. Particularly, no dogs— ever, ever again!" Freedom had come to me at last.

After all, I had raised two children, one husband, and five hundred cats, dogs, rabbits, ducks, turtles, and fish. I was now entering the "me" stage of living. For the first time in my life, I was on my own and looking forward to it. No more having to dash home after work because someone had to be fed or driven to Little League practice. My husband and I had divorced and gone our separate ways, my young adult children were off living their own lives, and my last remaining responsibility—our family dog—had died.

No more answering to or cleaning up after anyone or anything, especially a four-legged furry creature that enjoyed lifting his leg to spray every piece of upholstered furniture. Yep, free as a bird— that's what I wanted to be. No one to care for except myself. Such luxury.

And then I met Cody!

One afternoon while out walking, a greasy matted "ball of fur" suddenly ran past me, dragging his chain. In spite of the filth, I couldn't help but notice that there was something delightfully appealing about this little basketball-sized moppet. Maybe it was the fact that instead of actually running, he was moving along in a rather strange "rocking horse" sort of motion.

So I began chasing after him; once I was able to grab his chain, he finally stopped his mad dash long enough to turn his considerable energy into leaping up in the air, all the while trying to lick me. I was fascinated by the way he wagged his long tail like a flag in a windstorm.

But as cute as he was, there was absolutely no way I was going to touch the little urchin. So I walked him around and through the neighborhood in hopes of finding out where he belonged, while keeping him at an emotional, or so I thought, and physical distance.

In talking with several of the neighbors, I soon learned that he'd been living with an invalid woman and her two children and had been extremely neglected. And judging from his smell, I suspected that he was rarely, if ever, bathed. I was finally able to locate and return him to a young boy who owned him, and then without thinking, said, "If at any point you decide you can't keep this puppy, please call me."

WHAT WAS I THINKING?!!

I didn't give it a second thought until a few days later when the young boy's mother called me. She could no longer care for the dog and if my offer was still open, asked if Cody could please come live with me. Again, without a second thought, I responded: "Absolutely!"

WHAT WAS I THINKING?!!

Just in that short twenty- or thirty-minute walk around the neighborhood, without my even noticing I had formed a bond. I had indeed found where Cody belonged. Cody belonged with *me*.

That was fifteen years ago and I never once regretted my loss of freedom. Cody brought me such joy, devotion, laughter, and unconditional love that I can't imagine what I would have done without him. I guess I believed I would never have to find out.

This week, Cody's loving spirit left his body, and I now have the freedom that I so desperately wanted some years ago. I'm trying to learn how to live without my little friend, my protector, my special love buried deep within my heart. And I'm not doing such a good job of it. It turns out there is no real freedom, just an empty space I can't seem to fill, no matter how many tears I cry.

Jan O'Leary *is a mother, grandmother, day trader, real estate entrepreneur, and dog lover, who discovered the fascinating world of creative writing in a twelfth grade English class. In her words, "This discovery released a wounded bird from its cage, and after fifty years it's still flying free!" (253) 226-6163*

To My Golden Girl

by Bea Goldblatt

You are not gone,
Foxy. I see you everywhere.
In the Field today, you came over the ridge,
strutting and smiling with your tail wagging
in that way you have.
And I saw you in your son, your grandson, and granddaughter.
If the youngsters will be like you,
we shall be well-rewarded.
At home, you are everywhere.
On the cool tile entry, thumping your tail,
your dark eyes pouring out warmth and love.
You taught me so much in this twilight of our lives . . .
How to age with grace,
how to enjoy small pleasures,
how to hold each other close,
how to love life and friendships,
how to play, accept disfavors and triumphs,
and remain calm and strong.
And how to have pride, but not be proud.
You have left us all a legacy,
Foxy. You are not gone.

Bea Goldblatt *is a WWII veteran and former lab technician, physical therapist, editor, probation officer, and licensed clinical social worker. She has bred golden retrievers since 1954 and is a consultant for Golden Retriever Club of America. Bea enjoys writing stories and poetry.*

Chapter 4:
WAR & PEACE

The Girl with the Apple

by Herman Rosenblat

*A*ugust, 1942; Piotrkow, Poland. The sky was gloomy that morning as we waited anxiously. All the men, women, and children of Piotrkow's Jewish ghetto had been herded into a square. Word had gotten around that we were being moved. My father had only recently died from typhus, which had run rampant through the crowded ghetto. My greatest fear was that our family would be separated. "Whatever you do," Isidore, my eldest brother, whispered to me, "don't tell them your age. Say you're sixteen." I was tall for a boy of eleven, so I could pull it off. That way I might be deemed valuable as a worker. An SS man approached me, boots clicking against the cobblestones. He looked me up and down, then asked my age.

"Sixteen," I said. He directed me to the left, where my three brothers and other healthy young men already stood.

My mother was motioned to the right with the other women, children, sick and elderly people. I whispered to Isidore, "Why?" He didn't answer. I ran to Mama's side and said I wanted to stay with her. "No," she said sternly. "Get away. Don't be a nuisance. Go with your brothers." She had never spoken so harshly before. But I understood; she was protecting me. She loved me so much that just this once she pretended not to. It was the last I ever saw of her.

My brothers and I were transported in a cattle car to Germany. We arrived at the Buchenwald concentration camp one night weeks later and were led into a crowded barracks. The next day, we were issued uniforms and identification numbers. "Don't call me Herman anymore," I said to my brothers. "Call me 94983." I was put to work in the camp's crematorium, loading the dead onto a hand-cranked elevator. I, too, felt dead. Hardened. I had become a number.

Soon, my brothers and I were sent to Schlieben, one of Buchenwald's sub-camps near Berlin. One morning I thought I heard my mother's voice. "Son," she said softly but clearly, "I am sending you an angel."

Then I woke up. Just a dream. A beautiful dream. But in this place there could be no angels. There was only work. And hunger. And fear.

A couple of days later, I was walking around the camp, behind the barracks, near the barbed-wire fence where the guards could not easily see.

I was alone. On the other side of the fence, I spotted someone—a young girl with light, almost luminous curls. She was half-hidden behind a birch tree. I glanced around to make sure no one saw me. I called to her softly in German, "Do you have something to eat?" She didn't understand. I inched closer to the fence and repeated the question in Polish. She stepped forward. I was thin and gaunt, with rags wrapped around my feet, but the girl looked unafraid. In her eyes, I saw life. She pulled an apple from her woolen jacket and threw it over the fence. I grabbed the fruit, and as I started to run away I heard her say faintly, "I'll see you tomorrow."

I didn't believe she would come back. It was much too dangerous. But I returned anyway, the same time the next day. And there she was, the same girl. She moved tentatively from behind the tree and once again threw something over the fence. This time, it was a small hunk of bread wrapped around a stone. I ate the bread, gratefully and ravenously, wishing there had been enough to share with my brothers. When I looked up the girl was gone.

I returned to the same spot by the fence at the same time every day. She was always there with something for me to eat—a hunk of bread, or better yet, an apple. We didn't dare speak or linger. To be caught would mean death for us both. I didn't know anything about her—just a kind farm girl—except that she understood Polish. What was her name? Why was she risking her life for me? Hope was in such short supply, and this girl on the other side of the fence gave me hope, as nourishing in its way as the bread and apples.

Nearly seven months later, my brothers and I were crammed into a coal car and shipped to the Theresienstadt camp in Czechoslovakia. "Don't return," I told the girl that day. "We're leaving." I turned toward the barracks and didn't look back, didn't even say good-bye to the girl whose name I'd never learned, the girl with the apples.

We were at Theresienstadt for three months. The war was winding down and Allied forces were closing in, yet my fate seemed sealed. On May 10, 1945, I was scheduled to die in the gas chamber at 10:00 a.m. In the quiet of dawn, I tried to prepare myself. So many times death seemed ready to claim me, but somehow I'd survived. Now it was over. I thought of my parents. At least, I thought, we will be reunited. At 8:00 a.m., there was a commotion. I heard shouts and saw people running every which way through camp. I caught up with my brothers. Russian troops had liberated the camp!

The gates swung open. Everyone was running, so I did too. Amazingly, all of my brothers had survived; I'm not sure how. But I knew that the girl with the apples had been the key to my survival. In a place where evil seemed triumphant, one person's goodness had saved my life, had given me hope in a place where there was none. My mother had promised to send me an angel, and the angel had come.

Eventually, I made my way to England, where I was sponsored by a Jewish charity, put up in a hostel with other boys who had survived the Holocaust, and trained in electronics. Then I came to America, where my brother, Sam, had already moved. I served in the U.S. Army during the Korean War and returned to New York City after two years. By August 1957, I'd opened my own electronics repair shop. I was starting to settle in.

One day, my friend Sid, whom I knew from England, called me. "I've got a date. She's got a Polish friend. Let's double date."

A blind date? Nah, that wasn't for me. But Sid kept pestering me, and a few days later we headed up to the Bronx to pick up his date and her friend, Roma. I had to admit, for a blind date this wasn't so bad. Roma was a nurse at a Bronx hospital. She was kind and smart. Beautiful, too, with swirling brown curls and green, almond-shaped eyes that sparkled with life.

The four of us drove out to Coney Island. Roma was easy to talk to, easy to be with. Turned out she was wary of blind dates too! We were both just doing our friends a favor. We took a stroll on the boardwalk, enjoying the salty Atlantic breeze, and then had dinner by the shore. I couldn't remember having a better time.

We piled back into Sid's car, Roma and I sharing the backseat. As European Jews who had survived the war, we were aware that much had been left unsaid between us. She broached the subject. "Where were you," she asked softly, "during the war?"

"The camps," I said, the terrible memories still vivid, the irreparable loss I had tried to forget. But you never forget.

She nodded. "My family was hiding on a farm in Germany, not far from Berlin," she told me. "My father knew a priest, and he got us Aryan papers."

I imagined how she must have suffered too, with fear a constant companion. And yet here we were, both survivors, in a new world. "There was a camp next to the farm," Roma continued. "I saw a boy there, and I would throw him apples every day."

What an amazing coincidence that she had helped some other boy. "What did he look like?" I asked.

"He was tall. Skinny. Hungry. I must have seen him every day for six months."

My heart was racing. I couldn't believe it. This couldn't be . . . "Did he tell you one day not to come back because he was leaving Schlieben?"

Roma looked at me in amazement. "Yes."

"That was me!" I was ready to burst with joy and awe, flooded with emotions. I couldn't believe it. "My angel, I'm not letting you go," I said to Roma. And in the back of the car on that blind date, I proposed to her. I didn't want to wait.

"You're crazy!" she said. But she invited me to meet her parents for Shabbat dinner the following week. There was so much I looked forward to learning about Roma, but the most important things I always knew: her steadfastness, her goodness. For many months, in the worst of circumstances, she had come to the fence and given me hope. Now that I'd found her again, I could never let her go. That day, she said yes. And I kept my word: After nearly fifty years of marriage, two children, and three grandchildren, I have never let her go!

Herman Rosenblat is eighty-one years "young" and has been married to his beautiful wife, Roma, for fifty-four years. He is a Holocaust survivor who was held in concentration camps in Germany, Poland, and Czechoslovakia from age eleven to sixteen. "I am made of steel!" he proudly insists. He is a retired electrician whose passion lies in speaking to school-age children about making the most of their lives of freedom. hermro@aol.com

The War Secret

by Fred Owen

The Pacific Northwest sky was dark that November night in 1942. The air raid whistle at the main steam plant in our little town sounded the alert. We lowered all window shades and turned on only a few blue lights that wouldn't be visible from the air. Then we sat anxiously in our home, waiting to hear the drone of aircraft engines.

But the attack was a silent one.

We'd been warned of possible attacks by Japanese aircraft launched from submarines operating off Washington State's coast. We'd also been informed—with utmost secrecy—about the threat of attack from balloon-borne bombs that could float over the Pacific Ocean from Japan on prevailing winds. Those bombs would come directly to our town, we were told.

The authorities asked us not to speak of it to anyone if we found one of those bombs. Several of the balloon bombs did reach us, but they didn't explode. As more bombs fell into nearby agricultural fields, we kept it to ourselves. People whispered about them, but only within our homes.

Our commitment to silence left the Japanese to conclude that the bombs never reached American soil, and that the balloons were not worth sending. The bombs soon stopped landing in our fields.

The silence observed by farmers and other country folk in our corner of the nation made a difference in how the Japanese "warlords" pursued the war against America. Our secret never was revealed until the end of World War II.

Such secrecy—such cooperation and commitment to a common cause—was possible then. It was a different America.

__Fred Owen__ is an eighty-year-old human resource management consultant who helps government and private organizations set fair rates of pay for their employees. Fred actually experienced the World War II events described in his story. fsowen@comcast.net

Christmas 1945 at Camp 347

by Klaus Penning

At the time, I had no way of knowing that one day I'd be lucky enough to become an American citizen, living far from war, enjoying peacetime, married life, working at a great national park called Yosemite, and grateful for it all. But for now it was 1945, World War II, and I was a simple German soldier who found himself a prisoner of war in a Russian gulag camp known only by its number, 347.

The day started like any other there. We got up at six, dressed in our worn uniforms, washed our faces, went to an assembly area the size of a football field, found our places with our companies, and lined up in formation. After a freezing-cold wait of nearly one hour, the Russian commandant showed up with a German interpreter and our guards. Each company held 120 prisoners, and altogether, the camp held 1500 to 2000 German and Hungarian POWs. The prisoner-count took thirty to sixty minutes. Then it was back to our barracks where we were given our morning food ration—a bowl of cabbage soup and a small piece of bread. Once we'd eaten, the convoy of trucks was waiting for us.

Camp 347, near the Ukrainian town of Sanok, would be my first POW camp, and by far the worst. There was a lot of hatred between us and our captors, and our guards got away with not only beating us but with methodical starvation, as well. At least six hundred prisoners were not able to work because they looked like skeletons and were too weak. Today, of course, I know that the Germans treated Russian POWs not much better. Such is the nature of war, and how a country treats the soldiers of its enemy differs only in degree.

Every second day, a horse-drawn wagon left the camp with the bodies of the twenty to thirty POWs who'd died from one cause or another, but mainly from starvation. The bodies were buried outside the camp in mass graves by living prisoners, who, if they volunteered for the job, were rewarded with extra food and even some Vodka, which could, of course, keep a man alive.

Every Christmas since that year, I can't help but recall the first one I spent in Gulag 347. It was Christmas Day—we all knew this—but we boarded those trucks as always and were taken to our work site fifteen miles away. We were to build a dam for a railroad track. We dug the frozen ground with picks and shovels, broke up the dirt, carried it to the dam on a wooden stretcher, dumped it, then repeated this same process for what seemed like eternity. It was just another day of trying to survive, but it was hard not to think of home as the snow fell lightly around us. I wasn't even eighteen yet, and I'd already been away for two years.

Survival, though, depended upon thinking about food and dry clothes, not pretty snowflakes in the city where I'd grown up.

Our meal that night was a watery potato soup with a tiny piece of smelly fish that tasted awful, but we ate it, knowing it had protein in it and protein was life. After dinner, we sat as close as we could to the wooden stove, drying our coats if possible because they were also our blankets. I'd traded tobacco for some empty cement sacks to use as a mattress. We all did what we could.

At nine o' clock, the light was turned off and we were all alone with ourselves. Then a prisoner stood up and unexpectedly surprised us. Somehow, he had miraculously managed to produce a piece of a candle. He lit it, and set it on a wooden box next to the stove. What little conversation there had been now faded to silence as we all stared at the candle on the box.

I know we were all thinking the same thing. That if there was a light in the darkness, maybe there was some hope for us. Then suddenly out of the darkness came a voice singing "Silent night, holy night," and we all joined in singing this song of songs, grateful for the dark because it hid our tears. We were all longing for home, aching for our parents, wives, and children, and hoping we would live to see them again. When we finished, we wished each other the best and watched the candle until it burned itself out.

I have no way of knowing how many of those 120 POWs in my barrack survived—no one really does—but I do know what we all felt that night and how they must have also carried that Christmas with them into the future, however long that future was for each of them. I thank God that I was one of the lucky ones. I came home.

Klaus Penning *is eighty-three. He was born in Germany, served in the German Army during World War II, and was a POW in the Ukraine until 1949. In 1957, he emigrated to the U.S., where he worked as a farm laborer, operated his own sign business, and served on the Chamber of Commerce board. After retirement, he worked as a ski instructor and tour guide in Yosemite. Klaus27@gmail.com*

The "Dis-Orderly" Day

by Reverend Joseph Warner Skiles, Jr.

The day began like any other October day in our forward base in Germany during World War II. Five-thirty, rise and shine. Morning ablutions using our steel helmets. A quick trip in the back of a six-by-six truck to the mess tent. There we downed saddle-blanket-sized pancakes with axle-grease-type butter, coffee thick enough to make a spoon stand up, ready to meet whatever the day might bring. Then it was off to the operations tent for our briefing.

On this day, the operations officer was not his usual terse, laconic self. Instead, he seemed excited about some secret information he had received. "Two missions today," he finally announced. "We're going to breach the impregnable Siegfried Line on the first mission." Then he smiled. "I have a secret to tell you. The enemy has captured several of our tanks and taken the two-by-four cerise panels and put them on their own. Today's order is not company, not regiment, but a *general* order." He paused, took a deep breath, then unexpectedly shouted, "Destroy everything that moves!"

We all climbed into our planes and took off. Our instructions were to stay low—at treetop level—as we approached the pillboxes. As I neared my target, there in the open field was a horse. I was sick to my stomach as I followed orders and dropped my red targeting pipe squarely on the horse, then twitched my gauntleted trigger finger. The explosive shell had done its work and soon there was only red mist.

Again carrying out my orders as we neared the Siegfried Line, comprised of concrete pillboxes, I began firing at the extreme range of my cannons to prevent return fire from the machine guns. Within fifty yards of my target, I pressed the napalm bomb release with my thumb. In one and a half hours, the impregnable Siegfried Line had been breached.

The second mission began just as soon as the five-hundred-pound bombs could be attached under our aircraft's wings. Our target was a manufacturing city, heavily protected with numerous anti-aircraft guns; once again, our target approach was at low level. I was able to carry out my orders and skip-bombed both of my five-hundred-pounders into the main building.

I flew on, when all at once in front of me appeared a spidery railroad trestle across the river below. There on the trestle was a Toonerville Trolley-type train, the cars on which were much smaller than those we knew in America. Because it was moving, my orders were to destroy it, despite the fact that there were red crosses painted on all the cars. As I neared the target, I knew that one burst from me could topple the entire train into the river several hundred feet below.

But something prevented my trigger finger from twitching. I couldn't destroy a Red Cross train, even though I'd been told that the enemy was using them to move men and material. I saw a man peering out of one of the windows. As I passed over the train, our eyes met briefly over a distance of just a few feet.

Back at the base, my report included only the bombing and nothing more.

The rest of the story, as Paul Harvey would say, occurred six years later. One day, as I was reading my *Collier's* magazine, I came upon an article by a former war correspondent who wrote of being on a Red Cross train and looking out the window as a twin-tailed plane approached. He could see the pilot and braced himself because he was sure he was going to destroy the train.

I should have made an effort to correspond with that man, and regret that I did not. The only reason he was alive to write about the survival of the Red Cross train was because, for some unexplainable reason, I had disobeyed my orders of general destruction.

Reverend Joseph Warner Skiles, Jr. *(posthumously) was a World War II P-38 Army Air Corps pilot who flew over one hundred combat sorties in Europe. He was also an American Baptist minister for sixty years, plus a teacher and businessman. Rev. Skiles is survived by his wife, Genevieve, of sixty-five years, as well as by grandchildren and great grandchildren.*

The Greatest Generation

by Tom Brokaw

My friend Jack Hemingway, the firstborn of Ernest Hemingway, was raised in the tradition of his adventurous father, so it was only natural that when the war came along he'd be involved with the OSS. Jack also thought it was natural, when he parachuted into France behind enemy lines, to carry in his pack a tool of his favorite sport, a fly rod. When questioned about it before takeoff, he told a superior officer it was a radio antenna.

In his splendid book *The Misadventures of a Fly-Fisherman: My Life With and Without Papa,* Jack describes the few opportunities he had to use the fly rod in some lovely French streams before he was taken prisoner by the Germans. When I tell this story to other fishermen, they always seem to be more interested in the quality of the fishing than in Jack's fate as a prisoner. He seems to understand.

Gene Glick was a combat infantryman with the Army's 45th Division and personifies to this day the "dogface" Bill Mauldin so loved: tough, smart, and capable of finding an enduring truth in the worst possible situation. Glick, an Indiana native, was fighting in Alsace-Lorraine during the big push toward Germany, late in the fall of 1944. He says, "I'll never forget November eleventh, 1944, at eleven a.m. I dove into a slit trench." You dig a slit trench when you don't have time to dig a foxhole. It's about the size of your body—about two feet deep. There was a thin layer of ice. The shells were exploding all around him. He made a vow: "If I get out of this alive, anytime in the future, if it gets tough, I am going to remember November eleventh, 1944."

Glick survived the shelling and returned from the war to start what turned out to be one of the most successful residential companies in the United States, the Gene B. Glick Company. He's still on the job at the age of seventy-seven, although he's always willing to take a moment to tell you about his four daughters and his grandchildren. He took them to France in 1995 and had his grandchildren pose next to the headstone at a World War II cemetery so that, in his words, they would be reminded of "the tragedy of men not learning to live together in peace."

And what about that moment, November eleventh, 11 a.m., 1944? Gene Glick says that to this day, "It's like a guiding star. When things don't go right, when people disappoint me and projects don't work out, I think, Hey, Glick, November eleventh, 1944. No problem!"

From *The Greatest Generation* by **Tom Brokaw**, copyright © 1998 by Tom Brokaw. Used by permission of Random House, Inc.

Tom Brokaw *is a journalist, author, and popular award-wining television news anchor who has received numerous honors, accolades, awards, and honorary degrees for excellence in broadcast journalism. He is the author of* A Long Way from Home: Growing Up in the American Heartland *and* The Greatest Generation Speaks.

Vovochka

by Dora Klinova

When I first became a subscriber to the *San Diego Jewish Times* news magazine, one day the editors sent me a toy present—a small gray elephant—as a message of thanks and appreciation,

I recall that I didn't especially like it at first. It looked too gray and too dull, and I didn't know what to do with it. Then suddenly a sensation of warmth spread inside me, switching on something buried deep inside my head, "My God, it is my Vovochka!"

Suddenly, the year was 1942 and the Second World War was at its height.

We had managed to escape to Uzbekistan, far away from the German bombs, and we lived in a remote place not so far from the desert. I was a little girl. My only hat had been lost during the long evacuation. I remember how the hot sun burned me and that my nose was irritated, so Mama kept me in the shade. But I didn't have any toys to play with and was terribly bored.

Then one day, luck came to me in a muddy puddle. We found a toy, a little gray elephant, dirty and wet. It became my "son." I named him Vovochka, made clothes for him out of leaves and taught him good manners. I created an exotic hat, taking his big nose into consideration. Of course, the first lesson for my "son" was to always keep his hat on his head because the hot sun could burn his long nose as it did mine.

Once, when I couldn't find this hat, I immediately blamed him, yelling, "Vovochka, why have you lost your hat?" and slapped him for not being neat.

My poor little elephant . . . I was just a little child, sad and angry because of the war, because I missed my father who had already been killed at the front, because of the sadness of my mother, because of the many other "becauses" . . . I punched my toy so hard and yelled at it so loudly that I remember it now.

I played with my one and only toy during the whole war. Once, I decided that my "son" shouldn't have such a big nose, and since I already knew how to use scissors, I cut the elephant's trunk off. Bits of hay fell out of the little toy and I didn't have a "son" anymore.

Then more than sixty years passed.

I completely forgot about Vovochka. No, I didn't forget . . . Immediately this dull gray elephant in my hands became the brightest, warmest toy in my eyes. My childhood flooded back to me. I wanted to play with it as I had sixty years ago and to create the most magnificent hat for him. I found myself talking with him as I had in my childhood. I looked into his eyes; they seemed to be roguish, mischievous, and alive.

Now my Vovochka has become American and forgotten about his previous life in a muddy puddle. Now he has soft gray velvet skin and is dressed up in a cute blue T-shirt, made in America. He works at a respectable news magazine, *San Diego Jewish Times*, and represents it to the customers.

I am so glad for your great fortune, my Vovochka, but, please, please always remember the little girl from long ago who needed, loved, and played with you.

Dora Klinova *is an award-wining writer and poet whose works have been published in newspapers and magazines, and performed on stage. Her book,* A Melody from an Immigrant's Soul, *is the heartfelt story of a Russian Jewish immigrant.* dorishka2000@yahoo.com *or (619) 667-0925*

Graveyard Shift

by Patrick M. Flannery

Early in 1945, I was a radio-aerial gunner aboard a Navy bomber. At the time, we were in South America. My company received an order that we were to take our ancient plane, a PBM Mariner, up to an aircraft graveyard at the Panama Canal where they chopped up obsolete planes after removing valuable equipment.

At the beginning of the flight, I received my briefing. As the radioman, my assignment was to send a secret code to the canal when we were a hundred miles out. When we were fifty miles out, I was to send a second coded message. These security measures were mandatory precautions we had to take in order to enter the canal. If we didn't, we'd be shot down by American fighter pilots.

When we reached one hundred miles out, my captain called me on the intercom. "Flannery, send the first message."

"Aye, aye, sir," I answered, proud of the responsibility. I started to send the message, but, lo and behold, the sending key was not working. I knew I was in trouble, but I thought I'd be able to discover the trouble and fix it before I had to send the second message at fifty miles. But no luck. Nothing I tried worked, and I tried everything.

Then came the dreaded words from the pilot's sweating lips, "Flannery, send the second message. We're fifty miles away."

Embarrassed, and just a little terrified, I still didn't tell him we had a problem.

All at once, two American fighter planes, P-38s, came swarming all over us. My pilot assumed it was a routine welcome, but abruptly changed his mind when one of the P-38s fired his guns at us, though not close enough to cause us damage.

This woke my captain up. He bellowed in the intercom, "Flannery, did you send those messages?"

Even as I confessed that I hadn't, he was making a 180-degree turn because he knew that if the P-38s made one more pass at us, they'd have to bring us down with their guns. They couldn't take a chance on a hijacked Navy bomber putting a bomb in the canal and setting the war back months.

When we got on the ground, the pilot chewed me out, of course. My only defense was, "But, Captain, isn't that why we were taking these planes to the graveyard? Because nothing works on them anymore?"

He could have written me up as a wiseass, but he didn't. He was understanding. I may have gotten the longest chewing out of my life, but I also got to keep my first-class rating.

Patrick M. Flannery is an eighty-seven-year-old retired accountant. He and his wife of sixty-five years raised seven children and live in Elk Grove, California. As a former aviation radioman-aerial gunner, he would enjoy hearing from any of his shipmates from Naval Air Squadron 211 in WWII. (916) 684-3538

Chapter 5:
PORTRAITS IN TIME

Burnt Toast

by Kathe Kokolias

My mother—when she cooked at all—burned nearly everything she touched, starting with the breakfast toast. It wasn't her fault really. In her family of three sisters, my mother had been the one assigned the duty of cleaning. My aunt Kay baked. My aunt Madeleine shopped and helped my grandmother prepare their favorite dinners: moussaka, pastitsio, and lamb stew with fresh green beans.

It's not like my mother couldn't cook anything. She did learn to make creamy rice pudding and melt-in-your-mouth chocolate fudge, probably to beguile a boyfriend back in high school.

But her true love was cleaning the house. She concocted her own secret cleaning formulas to make our chandelier sparkle, all the while humming to herself as she took apart each hanging crystal. Yes, she was always happy in her work—as long as she wasn't interrupted and expected to cook a meal.

I recall how my brother and I would come home from school starving, and how she'd glare at us, saying, "You're hungry again?" As if making us breakfast should have been enough. Meanwhile, all day long she snacked on Fanny Farmer's chocolates—her personal rocket fuel—as she zipped around the house washing floors, vacuuming, and polishing the furniture till it gleamed.

But in the mornings she couldn't clean because she had to spend the time feeding us instead. My father would sit at the breakfast nook table, coffee cup in hand, reading the paper. His daily breakfast for most of his adult life, except when he was in the Marines during

World War II, consisted of coffee and two slices of lightly-buttered rye toast.

He stared at my mother hungrily as she ironed my skirt for school and talked with my grandmother on the telephone. Smoke rose from the toaster.

"Not again, Eleni!" he bellowed, using my mother's Greek name.

My grandmother had called to talk about last night's dream and she and my mother were trying to make sense of it. I grew up thinking that the women in every family talked together each morning, sharing and interpreting their dreams—dreams that held as much credence as the morning news on WTRY.

"You dreamed of a knife," my mother was saying into the phone, "so that means a man is coming. Who could be coming to visit? Uncle Tim or some relative from Fitchburg?" Mom told my grandmother that she'd better start cooking something special because nine times out of ten, someone would ring the doorbell, suitcase in hand, just in time for dinner.

"Helen!" My father had switched back to English, his tone more insistent. "I have to leave in five minutes! Could I *please* have something to eat?"

Mom bid a hasty good-bye to my grandmother, whispering that she'd call her back as soon as my father went out the door.

Maybe that's why I've never enjoyed breakfast. Each morning I struggle to consume something to fill the void, although nothing seems quite right, nothing really satisfies. For twenty-five years I've been married to a man who, unlike my mother, *loves* to cook and excels at it. In fact, breakfast is his favorite meal to prepare and he always tries to tempt me with a variety of delectable dishes: Fluffy French toast drizzled with Vermont maple syrup, golden pancakes that fill the entire frying pan, and which he flips with the expertise of a Culinary Institute graduate, or opulent omelets oozing with onions, green peppers, and melting Monterey Jack cheese.

I know I'm very lucky to have such a wonderful caring husband, but the truth is that what satisfies me the most is a piece of toast—slightly burned, please.

Kathe Kokolias *is a photographer, painter, and published writer who lives in Colonie, NY, and Ixtapa, Mexico. She is the author of* What Time Do the Crocodiles Come Out?, Spandex & Black Boots, *and* A Woman's World Again. *kathekokolias@aol.com or www.kathekokolias.com*

Making the Grade

by Irene Miller

"You never have to be sorry for what you didn't say." My mother drummed this into my head at an early age and it may have helped me hold my tongue at a crucial moment in the life of a certain ten-year-old.

I had been teaching fifth grade in Ridgefield, Connecticut, for about two months when the report card period ended. Tired as I was on that Sunday evening, I forced myself to transfer the marks from my record book to the report cards. Then I decided to break for a cup of tea. Returning to the task, I inadvertently copied the last boy's marks onto another boy's report card. I continued on correctly, finishing the cards in time to distribute them at the close of school the following day.

My fifth grade was mostly made up of average children with a few very bright and a few rather slow learners, some of whom could have done better if I could have figured out the magic needed to motivate them. One of these was John Morton. John seemed unwilling to sit still very long, pay attention very long, or work independently. His anecdotal record bore this out, and one after another of his teachers had dismissed him as immature and hopelessly unmotivated, with the marks to prove it.

Two days of parent conferences followed the distribution of report cards and I always found it interesting, even surprising, to meet the parents and talk with them individually. When John Morton's young mother came in she greeted me with outstretched hand and the warmest smile. "Mrs. Miller, I'm so glad to meet you!" she enthused. "I can't tell you how thrilled we were with John's report card. I

CRIED when I saw it. John's father is on a business trip but I phoned him to tell him about it and he was so happy."

She ran on in her talkative way, telling me about John's babyhood, his early childhood, his troublesome younger brother and sister, his difficulties with all his previous teachers, never pausing to notice my complete astonishment. Her twenty minutes were soon over, interrupted by the arrival of the next parent. Mrs. Morton squeezed my hand warmly. Then off she went, leaving me completely bewildered and not a little uneasy. What was she talking about?

The first thing I did when classes resumed was to collect the report cards and examine John's marks. It became clear that I had given John the same excellent marks as Bobby Martin on the line above him in my record book. Fortunately no one had been given John's marks. That fateful break for a cup of tea must have been the explanation. Now what was I to do? Report it to the principal? Call John's mother and tell her it was all a mistake? Offer my apologies to John? Offer my resignation to the school board?

As I often did when I was stymied, I went across the hall to ask the advice of older, wiser, witty, and cynical Don Oberon. Years of wrestling with bureaucratic paper work and meager salary increases had given Don a jaundiced view of parents, teachers and certainly administrators. He listened with a slight smile, rolling his eyes at my description of my conference with Mrs. Morton. What seemed like a major problem to me was quickly put into perspective.

"Explain what? Are you kidding? Say NOTHING!" advised my mentor. I decided to take his advice. It happened to coincide with my mother's maxim. I hurried back to my room across the hall.

In my class that morning was a complete stranger named John Morton. No more the boy who dawdled with his assignment and talked ceaselessly with his neighbor. John was suddenly tall in his seat, eyes alert, the first to get out his text, the first to begin his work. He was suddenly seeing himself as a completely new person—a success, a scholar, the pride of his parents, a serious student—it was absolutely amazing!

This was not just a nine-day wonder. It continued all year. In fact, John's school work improved significantly as did his marks, which only reflected his hard work and new work attitudes. That incident helped me to really understand the importance of self-esteem in children. The only thing I did for John was to keep my mouth shut.

From *Making the Grade* with the kind permission of author **Irene Miller**, copyright owner.

Irene Miller *joyfully recalls her years of teaching in New York State, Connecticut, and California. She is a widow and grandparent who lives in Minnesota when not traveling. Irene is the founder of a writer's group and cherishes the many precious friendships that result when seniors share their memoirs.*

Saturday Afternoons at the Movies

by Dorothy E. Demke

The 1930s marked the worldwide economic downturn known as "The Great Depression." There was no television, but there was radio. And we had movies. Almost everybody went to the movies. Salaries were small, but with careful budgeting it was possible—almost necessary.

There was always a double feature shown, plus a cartoon and newsreel, "The Eyes and Ears of the World." I also remember a sing-along. We followed the bouncing ball as words to patriotic tunes, popular ballads, and tunes like "Old MacDonald" appeared on the movie screen. Nobody checked to find out when a movie started. You arrived whenever you could and stayed until the film reached the point where you came in. Theaters were decorated like glamorous palaces, with gilt and columns. Once inside, a uniformed usher with a flashlight and acne conducted you to your seat.

When my brother Alan and I were small, we were taken to the movies every Saturday afternoon. I was most impressed by the bride of Frankenstein. She was beautiful with her dark lipstick and her huge hairdo set off by two electrical-looking silver stripes. Other people gasped in horror, while I gasped in admiration. I was only five years old, but I recognized and appreciated style when I saw it.

In the late thirties, Saturday afternoons were when kiddie matinees were scheduled. Fifteen cents got you in and you could spend five hours sitting in the dark under the flickering ray of the projector, eating enormous five-cent candy bars. A triple feature was usually shown, perhaps a "Tom Mix" or "Buck Rogers in the 25th Century" movie where science fiction creatures with enormous collars were battled. Sometimes they included a light-hearted love story that was set in a home far more elegant than the spartan homes of most of the folks in the audience. Serials and cartoons filled the rest of the time. It was heaven for us children. Even the ceiling of the theater was decorated with a celestial scene.

On one particular Saturday, Alan and I walked the ten blocks to the theater, and as usual, I was made to walk three paces behind him. He had been told to take me but was damned if he'd be seen with his younger—and most embarrassing—sister. Once inside, I was permitted to sit behind him. In those days, children were seated in the children's section, which was supervised by a matron, a situation mandated by law, but which we as kids all deplored.

The movie was about Richard III, loosely based on Shakespeare's play about that oily, scheming, ambitious fiend. The ruthless one was played by Basil Rathbone. But Boris Karloff, as Frankenstein in England, supplied the greatest horror.

Karloff, the grunting troglodyte—the stiff-legged bozo—was the designated hit guy for the man who would be king. All rightful successors to the throne had to be whacked until it became Richard's turn. So in one horrendous scene, the monster stood on the edge of a balcony, poised to toss the innocent little prince over the railing. Just then, Alan shouted at the top of his lungs, "HE'S GONNA HEAVE!"

All the startled patrons in the theater turned toward us in that one ruined moment. And so did the usher with his flashlight! We sat there staring straight ahead, trying to appear innocent. But we soon found ourselves outside the theater, walking home in the pale winter sunshine, short of at least one feature film, several chapters of exciting serials, plus five cartoons. Darn that Alan!

Dorothy E. Demke (*posthumously*) *grew up in New York City, where she developed a love for the visual, performing, and cultural arts. She later enjoyed studying dance. Dorothy and her husband purchased a failing bakery in Claremont, CA, and transformed it into an award-winning success, known for its "real" butter, eggs, and flour, and the early introduction of the croissant. Dorothy died last year.*

The Soda Jerk

by Bea Goldblatt

During my high school years, the small shopping district in our community was pretty much limited to Avenue J. Here, along one street was our butcher (who sold only fish on Fridays), our baker, grocer, and drugstore with its ice cream fountain and high bar stools. And there behind the counter, presiding over the shakes, sundaes, malts, ice cream sodas, and syrups was the "soda jerk."

Sally, Dottie, and I were closest best friends. We three not only walked to school together, played together, had the Candy Club together, and enjoyed Coney Island together, but when we were eleven or twelve, we three "loved the soda jerk together" all at the same time.

As soon as school was out each day, we'd rush home to change from our middy blouses and blue serge skirts into our "wash" dresses. Middy blouses were white with a squared sailor collar in the back and a small band to hold a red tie in the front. Middies were adapted from the uniform of the midshipman and worn outside a blue pleated skirt. Although we were only obliged to wear these outfits on Friday Assembly Days, most of us wore them daily as our school clothes. Otherwise, we wore cotton wash dresses, which were exactly that. Dresses that were washed and ironed, as opposed to silk or satin dresses that you'd wear to a restaurant, the movies, or when going shopping with your mother.

So as soon as we had changed into our wash dresses we'd meet at Sally's house and walk down the street together, full of girlish giggles, to the drugstore on Avenue J. Then while we sat upon the high stools, we'd all three ogle the blushing high school boy of sixteen or seventeen who worked there part-time and was known as the soda jerk. Not that *he* was a jerk. It was just the name given to the person who pulled—or jerked—the fountain handle to add carbonated water (fizz) to an ice cream soda. For some unknown reason, his was a highly coveted position.

Sally, Dottie, and I would each order a "black and white" soda, made of one or two scoops of vanilla ice cream, chocolate syrup, and sparkling seltzer water. We'd take our time sipping our sodas slowly, all the while trying to catch the eye of the soda jerk, doing all we could to attract his attention by talking loudly about school friends and so forth.

A "black and white" cost ten cents, so since the allowance we received was probably fifty cents, we spent all of our allowance money in those days just watching the soda jerk. He was pleasant but of course paid no special attention to any of us, for he was only interested in high school girls. So there you have it—the simple vignette of three happy, giggling girls at the soda fountain on Avenue J, each in love with the soda jerk back in the hard-to-remember days of early innocence.

Bea Goldblatt *is a WWII veteran and former lab technician, physical therapist, editor, probation officer, and licensed clinical social worker. She has bred golden retrievers since 1954 and is a consultant for Golden Retriever Club of America. Bea enjoys writing stories and poetry.*

The Butcher

As told to Roxie Parks by Amaly Louise Heaney

The center of all activity in our tiny house was the kitchen. With gas for cooking, hot water from one of those new heating tanks, and the icebox in the corner, the kitchen was clearly the entertainment center as well as my culinary castle. Pillars separated the kitchen and living room with cupboards beneath them. Two small bedrooms completed the home, totaling eight hundred square feet in all.

Tom and I had moved into our new home in April 1914. With us came my three boys, Albert, Willy, and Charles from my first husband, Art, making an instant family for Tom. Art had died five years earlier, and Tom took to my sons so well that they soon called him "Dad." Tom had sisters, brothers, and a mother whom we called Mother Heaney. My boys, my new husband, and my new home all made me very happy. My heart was filled with gladness!

Yes, we were happy but poor, for Tom's earnings at Pacific Electric only amounted to two dollars a week. One dollar of that money went for medication for Willy, who had been sickly all of his life, and the remainder was for household expenses. Now with my new family and new house, I was to make my first dinner for Mother Heaney. As her new daughter-in-law, I was determined to put on a good show. Mother Heaney was well known for her stern behavior and curt remarks, so what was I to do? Well, off to the store I went with twenty-five cents in hand and a dream to make a good impression on her.

But as I looked at all the meat under the glass, I cried. Oh, how I wished I could afford a nice steak or roast that I could slow-cook with vegetables and make a delicious dinner! The butcher, who knew my story well, moved closer to me. He understood that making ends meet on half a salary for the sake of a sick child was my first priority. We housewives always valued his advice and kind friendship. On special occasions, he often gave us free liver, kidney, or giblets if he had an oversupply.

The wise butcher advised me to buy a pound of weenies for ten cents and slice them real thin so they looked like far more than a pound. Then, I was to fry the weenies with chopped garlic while stirring in the white sauce to add flavor to the gravy. And to impress my guest, he suggested I buy store-bought bread for another five cents. Yes, I knew I could complete this dinner with lettuce picked from my garden that day, oil and vinegar dressing, and a fresh squash casserole. So I marched home straight away with these treasured thoughts in my mind, a pound of weenies, a loaf of bread, and some change in my pocketbook.

I did just as the butcher said, and also used the secret of serving everything in smaller dishes to make the food portions appear larger.

First, I toasted the bread and let my guests spoon the weenie gravy onto the toast themselves. Then, I served a garden squash casserole smothered in the fat that I always saved in the can at the back of the stove. My salad contained dandelion greens, fresh mustard leaves, and new leaf lettuce. I was feeling happy and proud because my dinner was tasty and impressive, with plenty to eat for everyone.

Now Mother Heaney's nature was not to receive anything without making a mean-spirited remark afterwards. And sure enough, the next time she saw me she told me off by saying, "The next time you invite me over for dinner, Louise, please leave out the garlic! Don't try to hide it, dear. I can always taste it. I will always know." Ooh, I'm much too timid to fight back, but deep down inside I was determined to develop a secret plot to fool her.

So back to the butcher I went, whimpering my story to him.

He just smiled and told me to simply boil an egg or two till hard, then cut up the whites just as small as I would cut up the garlic. And the next time she came for dinner, I should add small chopped egg whites to the food I was serving. "Just sit back and wait for what comes next," he said, winking. I did exactly what the butcher told me to do.

And so the next time Mother Heaney came for supper, I served my famous "Chili on Waffles," a dish my husband, Tom, and children have always loved. I fixed it as usual, but instead of putting chopped garlic in the chili, I diced the egg whites thin and small so as to resemble garlic, adding them to the chili last. Then I sat back and watched for what would come next.

Mother Heaney ate her dinner, then suddenly pushed her chair back and sternly said, "I told you not to put garlic in my food, Louise. I can smell and taste it no matter how small you cut it!"

"Did you like the dinner?" I asked quietly.

Coyly, she replied, "Except for the garlic, it was okay."

I carefully said, ever so calmly, barely able to contain myself, "There is no garlic in the chili."

Well, Mother Heaney loudly belted out, "Do you think I'm blind? I can see it right there!" She pointed to the tiny white spots submerged in the chili pot.

"That white you see is egg white. I merely chopped egg white into my chili. There's no garlic," I calmly replied.

At that point, Mother Heaney bellowed a great big, "Well!" then abruptly stood up with another loud "humph" and left.

Tom was surprised by my actions, but he fully supported me and I could see he was sort of laughing too. Mother Heaney didn't come back for an awfully long time. Thanks to the butcher, I made my point, earned my husband's support, and won a small battle that I needed to fight—I mean needed to plot!

Roxie Parks *is a sixty-seven-year-old retired housekeeper, caregiver, and professional clown who actively serves her family, community, and*

Jan Fowler

church in Yucaipa, California. Amaly Louise Heaney, her maternal grandmother, helped raise her in the small family homestead. Roxie is writing memories of her grandma's life for her children and grandchildren.
<u>*craftyroxie@verizon.net*</u>

Love, Uncle Marty

by Martin S. Goldberg

Dear Steve,

I know that present times often look tough, and for the fainthearted, could even be catastrophic. So now let me relate the tale of a courageous mother who found herself abandoned in Chicago with two very young boys during the winter of 1930. Her sons were only one and six years old.

Without a whimper, she took a job playing piano in a speakeasy until she could find work in a better environment. Her search took two years, but she did eventually land a job with a music publisher in New York City where she then moved with her two children. A small apartment in a tough westside neighborhood became their home. One side of their building faced Columbus Avenue where the Ninth Avenue El trains ran all night long.

This young mother's pay at the music publisher was quite low, so in order to remedy the situation she also began working as an accompanist in nightclubs—all in addition to her job at the music publisher by day. Her work hours in the clubs began at nine in the evening and lasted until two in the morning. This brave mother maintained this grueling schedule for several years until she earned enough money to send her two sons to military school.

Somehow, this extraordinary lady also managed to take her sons to see the circus, rodeos, Broadway shows, an occasional opera, as well as boxing matches, which included Police Athletic League (PAL) bouts staged on the streets.

Her sons were able to see her perform in every nightclub where she worked and often watched her from the wings while she also played piano for vaudeville singers. In addition to accompanying top singers, I might add that she became a vocal arranger and also a successful songwriter along the way.

During the height of the Depression, one had to become a very competent shopper in order to make limited money stretch. This lady would walk extra blocks and go out of her way to save money even on small items, a habit that continued into her later years. Her attitude was that all these extra hikes helped to keep her in great physical condition.

Oh, and did I mention that she also belonged to a group called the Bedside Network, an organization that performed for disabled vets at the veterans' hospitals after the war? She volunteered to entertain at these hospitals twice a week through the 1980s until shortly before her death. There was no compensation or extra recognition for this work, just the heartfelt satisfaction of bringing entertainment to these veterans.

Her two sons grew up without ever hearing their mother moan about life being tough, or complain about not being able to afford things beyond her financial reach.

This remarkable lady was the mother of your father and me.

Love,
Uncle Marty

Martin S. Goldberg is a retired Ohio trial attorney who graduated from Ohio State University Law School. He is also a combat veteran from World War II. He began writing following his retirement in 2002 and has now completed a mystery. (760) 773-4773

Priceless Gifts

by Shirley Huston

Throughout my childhood my father gave me many special gifts, not one of which was related to money. As a matter of fact, they all came from *lack* of money.

My father's gifts to me were IOUs written on little slips of folded paper that bore his signature and that read, "IOU . . ." followed by whatever it was he wished he could give me but couldn't afford at the time. Some examples of the priceless gifts I found in the folded creased scrap papers were:

Humility . . . not being ashamed to admit he didn't have the money at the time.

Honesty . . . not covering up with a substitute.

Integrity . . . making a pact with me and promising to fulfill it.

Faith in himself . . . that he would one day be able to redeem the IOUs.

Belief in *me* . . . that I would understand and accept his promise.

Patience . . . to wait for things promised with an open heart and belief that they would come.

Love . . . learning that love is the most important gift of all.

Over time, these IOUs gradually became gifts in themselves because somehow he always managed to redeem them. Often, that took many months, but I treasured the IOUs with my dad's signature dearly and now know why. Through them, he gave me wisdom.

Through my father, I learned not to be afraid to give a promise to someone you trust and, of course, the importance of keeping that promise. But the greatest lesson from the IOUs is the importance of now making it my mission to pass them on.

Shirley Huston *is a retired marketing executive who "unretired" to serve as executive director of a trade association for thirteen years. She has written a newspaper column, plus numerous media and corporate commercials and promotional materials. Shirley serves as literary agent and editor for several budding authors.* <u>*shuston.litagent@verizon.net*</u>

The Wedding Present

by Anne J. Basile

I remember the day when the Dormeyer Electric Food Fixer arrived. Robert and I had received it as a wedding gift in 1945, but at the time it was delivered, we were packing to leave for the student life at Iowa State College and just weren't able to take it with us.

In those days, my cooking skills were rather limited anyway—although I could boast of making delicious fudge—but it wasn't until a few years later when we began to raise a family that I resolved to become a good cook. It was then that I unpacked the Dormeyer Mixer, Model Number 4200, which had been safely stored with Robert's parents for the last four years. An enclosed pamphlet boasted of ten recipe-tested speeds, as well as such features as *"It's a Grinder, It's a Juicer, It's a Mixer!"* It wasn't long till I discovered that the mixer truly *was* the most useful appliance in my kitchen.

The grinding, juicing, and mixing attachments that came with it simplified food preparation. I practiced the recipes from the booklet and was especially proud of my first cake. Encouraged, I then tackled complete meals. From the juicer extractor, delicious foamy juices poured out. From the grinder, raisins, oranges, and nuts were combined into special loaves. Whipped toppings were a breeze. Even neglected leftovers became tasty meals. I learned that life in the kitchen could be rewarding and even fun with the help of my handy mixer.

In time, our three daughters also discovered the magic of the mixer. Everyone looked forward to preparing special treats for the holidays. We were extremely proud of the girls when they won first prize for an elegant gingerbread house.

Only once did we have a problem involving the food fixer when Robert attempted to straighten the blades. Unfortunately, he had neglected to pull out the plug and pushed the power button by mistake. Trying to remain calm, he called out to me, "Anne, would you please come here?" I was down in the basement folding the wash, so I casually answered, "Just a minute, dear." But when he called a second time, I recognized the urgency in his voice and realized that he must be in serious trouble. So I quickly ran upstairs and found him bent over the mixer with both hands trapped in the blades. It took longer than expected to extricate him, in spite of his urging me to please hurry. I finally realized he was worried about spoiling his "fix-it" image with our daughters. Suppressing a smile, I managed to free him before they ever arrived home from school. Fortunately, he only had dents in his fingers; it was just his pride that was hurt.

Sixty anniversaries later, my wonderful faithful fixer still sits in its accustomed place under the sink, ready to be of service. Our grandchildren marvel that anything so old remains in such great shape and still works! We tell them it operates on the same philosophy *we* do; namely, that it's better to *wear* out than rust out.

***Anne J. Basile**, now in her mid-eighties, was a librarian at Davis College in Toledo, Ohio. She began writing her memoirs several years ago for her children, grandchildren, and great grandchildren. Anne is both founder and president of her local chapter of the Church and Synagogue Library Association. (419) 882-1610*

Memories of Bubie

by Hilda K. Phillips

I remember being seated on the couch, legs dangling, my hands on my lap, smiling and waiting for Grandma. We called her Bubie, but I know that her real name was Riva Manne Schweidel. Even at five years old, I wanted to be especially proper, ever so ladylike.

Finally, Bubie came over and sat down next to me. Then ever so gently and lovingly, she told me she would be going away, just for a few days. Bubie's English was easy for me to understand, although every once in awhile she'd intersperse it with some Yiddish words. "Ich daft gaen to Brooklyn."

Turning away from me slightly, I suddenly saw that my Bubie's eyes were swelling up with tears. Even being a child, I somehow sensed that leaving me was just as traumatic for *her* as it was for me. Deep down inside, I desperately wanted to believe that I was extra special to her.

"Bubie," I sobbed too, "why are crying? Why are you so sad? Why are you going to Brooklyn and leaving me?

"Who will wash my hair and tell me, 'Mamala, the ends have to be cut, just a bisel; it makes the hair grow thicker'?

"Who will be there to chop the fish for Friday and ask me, 'Mamala, does it need more pepper? Does it need more salt?' "Just a little more pepper," I would answer as I devoured the delicious fresh fish.

"Who will be there to make the pots and pans shine like mirrors? No one can ever do it the way my Bubie does!" I said.

"Who will be there to light the Shabbos candles with Mamma and me?

"Who will be there to make the Shabbos noodles for the chicken soup?

"Who will be there to show me how to use the thimble when I sew?"

Oh, how I tried to manipulate and lovingly make her stay. I even asked, "Don't you love me anymore?"

As far as I can remember, my Bubie was the only person at the time to whom I had ever even spoken the word "love."

"Mamala," she replied, "I have to go visit my son, your uncle Sam. I also want to see my granddaughter, Sylvia, and my grandson, Sheldon. Of course, there is my daughter-in-law, Anne."

It was then that I first learned that my mother and uncle Sam were twins and that Sylvia and Sheldon were my first cousins. Deep down inside, I had always wished to be a twin. I found a pair in a coloring book, and since I did have a younger sister, I would look at her as I pranced and danced about the house singing, "We are twinees from Yugoslavia!" I was learning global culture.

I can still see little me at the open window, watching her leave and crying out, "Bubie, don't go, don't go, I promise I will be a good girl!"

"*Du bist* a good girl," my Bubie told me, but she still had to leave me.

And so she did.

Hilda K. Phillips *is eighty-six years old and a retired educator. She remains active with library volunteer work, serving on the Senior Advisory Committee of Rancho Cucamonga, CA, and was a district representative for the San Bernardino, California Volunteer Council. She performs with two choirs and enjoys writing poetry. (909) 945-3627*

Did You Hear Me?

by Donna Kicak

Our mom is ninety-six years old and continues to be a very loving and proud woman. My sister Kay and I cherish and love her dearly, but feel that she can be stubborn. Consider this example . . .

For the past ten years, Kay and I have been concerned about Mom's hearing. We really wanted her to get a hearing aid, but never quite knew how to approach the subject without offending her.

But one evening a few years ago, while Kay was here on a visit from her home in Texas, we decided it was time we let Mom know how we felt. We would lovingly, but firmly, point out how much conversation she has been missing out on without the benefit of a hearing aid. And so, as we all sat around the dining room table after a relaxing dinner, we decided it was the perfect time to bring up the subject. So here we go!

Our question to Mom: "Mom, have you ever thought about getting a hearing aid?"

Mom's reply: "No, I hear just fine, but you girls should speak louder."

Our reply: "Mom, if you won't consider trying a hearing aid, we are going to stop calling because you never hear our whole conversation and we keep repeating ourselves."

Mom's reply: "That will be just fine. Just remember to write me a letter."

And so till this day, our loving, proud, and STUBBORN mom does not have a hearing aid. So, what do we do? We talk louder, repeat ourselves, do not send letters, but we still call!

Donna Kicak *is a mother, grandmother, and wife who has been happily married for forty-seven years. She retired as vice president of Kicak & Associates, Inc., a civil engineering firm, and now devotes her leisure time to caring for her home, spending quality time with family and friends, reading, and solving crossword puzzles.*

Stop, Charley, Stop!

by Jim Craw

When I first settled in the small citrus-growing town of Redlands, California, in 1948, I began working for the California Water and Telephone Company on one of their many heavy construction crews. One of our first job assignments was to remove a row of twelve-inch square wooden poles along Terracina Boulevard, a rather wide street that borders on orange groves on one side. I might add that these poles were quite sizeable and also extremely heavy. They measured eighteen or twenty feet tall and had cross-arms that were attached by lag screws only.

Once the wires had been removed from the poles, Charley Wilson, our foreman, was walking alongside the line shaking each pole individually to see how easily it would come out of the ground. But when he shook one of the poles, the cross-arm suddenly came loose and fell, unexpectedly hitting Charley a glancing blow on the back of his head. Obviously stunned, sore, and apparently scared, Charley dropped down to his knees, then suddenly rose up again, only to begin running deep into the groves.

One of our crew members, Jim, saw all this happen and with the rest of us following, chased Charley into the grove yelling, "Stop, Charley, stop!" But the only answer we heard from Charley, was *"Blankety-blank, you Blankety-blank . . . !"*

Finally Charley did stop because he fell to the ground. Once we were able to reach him, Jim asked, "Charley, why in the world did you run off like that?"

"I thought one of you 'so-and-sos' hauled off and hit me with a lag wrench," he yelled. "And I wasn't about to give you a second chance!"

As it turned out, Charley was a very lucky man that day. For if the cross-arm had hit the very *top* of his head, it could have easily killed him. And if he had been hit by any of the lag screws in the arm, they too could have caused severe injury or lasting damage.

I worked that crew many more years and never knew anyone who ever disliked Charley, let alone ever wanted to harm him. But I'll never forget the day when Charlie mistakenly misunderstood the circumstances, tore off in a panic, and made a sudden getaway deep into the orange groves.

Jim Craw *holds the title of the longest living member of Redlands Footlighters Theatre, where he has performed in and directed many plays, as well as served on their board of directors. After leaving the California Water & Telephone Co., Jim worked for Marketeer Manufacturing, which assembled one of the first electric vehicles built specifically as a golf cart.*

MiLouise

by Joanne Pottier

I will miss my dear and special friend, MiLouise. It's difficult for me to believe she won't be with us to enjoy another floral season. Her passing came as such a surprise because her eighty-seven-year-old-heart always seemed so lively and young. MiLouise was full of curiosity and spunk, and I loved the way she cheered me with her humor.

There were times when I thought my own heart would fall each time I watched her tottering her way down the steep bank between our homes. With arms outstretched for balance, she resembled a small plane in a windy landing, but had every confidence and determination to stand on her own. She never fell once. It was much the same way she approached most things in life.

One time, at Molbak's Home & Garden Center, where she loved to take me on Tuesdays to offer me her senior discount, when a clerk asked us if we were mother and daughter, she replied, "No, we're neighbors and *really* good friends." The clerk was visibly moved and laughed aloud with us while MiLouise gave me a great big hug. I'll miss those spontaneous "just because" hugs that I received from her so often.

MiLouise's China stories demonstrated her bold sense of adventure and daring curiosity. One day, while on her way to rendezvous with her husband, Ben, in China at the end of the war, she saw a road that she opted to follow as a shortcut to their meeting. But when this road turned out to be a highly restricted security area for authorized personnel only, she was quickly whisked away in a jeep—all to Ben's startled astonishment. Later, she simply explained, "Well, I just wanted to know what was down that road," nonchalant about her circumstances in unstable postwar Red China.

Our "Street of Dreams" multimillion dollar fund-raising-home-tour outings stand out as the most fun, with garden shows a close second. Once, when she gazed up at a long spiraling staircase leading to the second floor, she pleaded, "Now if you'd have the patience to help me up there, I know I could make it." So we slowly made the climb and after her successful conquest, she looked down and laughed. "Oh my, now wouldn't it be fun to slide down the banister!" On another occasion when I said I didn't know if we were still in the master bedroom or had moved into the entertainment room, she joked, "Well, you know the master bedroom can be the best entertainment room of all!"

MiLouise was never afraid to ask questions and remained a research librarian long after retirement. In fact, any expression of interest in any topic whatsoever would send her into an indefatigable search for information. She sure didn't need the internet—her own search mode rivaled Google. Our house was always filled with proof of her research: newspaper clippings, phone numbers, magazines, book referrals. MiLouise was well read and blessed with such a fertile mind that her knowledge spanned topics ranging from gardening to world events.

And she was a most refreshing two-way conversationalist. If she asked you how you were, she sincerely wanted to hear the answer. She lived my own experiences vicariously and made me feel that I was important to her life. There are very few people like my friend, MiLouise. I will treasure her special friendship forever.

***Joanne Pottier** is a fifty-seven-year-old retired meteorologist who co-owns a consulting business with her husband near Seattle, Washington. She enjoys running, gardening, entertaining, reading, and the great outdoors. Mostly, Joanne loves it all! jpottier@comcast.net*

Chapter 6:
HOT DOGS & MUSTARD
FOR SPORTS FANS

Every Second Counts

by Lance Armstrong

M y friend Lee Walker says I got "pitched back." What he means is, I almost died, and possibly even did die a little, but then I got pitched back into the world of the living. It's as good a description as any of what happened. I was twenty-five when cancer nearly killed me: advanced choriocarcinoma spread to my abdomen, lungs, and brain and required two surgeries and four cycles of chemotherapy to get rid of. I wrote an entire book about death, called *It's Not About the Bike*, about confronting the possibility of it, and narrowly escaping it.

"Are you sure?" I asked the doctor.

"I'm sure."

"How sure?"

"I'm very sure."

"How can you be so sure?"

"I'm so sure that I've scheduled you for surgery at 7 a.m. tomorrow."

Mounted on a light table, the X-ray showed my chest. Black meant clear; white meant cancer. My chest looked like a snowstorm.

What I didn't and couldn't address at the time was the prospect of life. Once you figure out you're going to live, you have to decide how to, and that's not an uncomplicated matter. You ask yourself: *now that I know I'm not going to die, what will I do? What's the highest and best use of myself?"* These things aren't linear, they're a mysterious calculus. For me, the best use of myself has been to race in the Tour de France, the most grueling sporting event in the world.

Every time I win another Tour, I prove that I'm alive—and therefore that others can survive, too. I've survived cancer again, and again, and again, and again. I've won four Tour titles, and I wouldn't mind a record-tying five. That would be some good living.

But the fact is that I wouldn't have won even a single Tour de France without the lesson illness. What it teaches is this: pain is temporary. Quitting lasts forever.

To me, just finishing the Tour de France is a demonstration of survival. The arduousness of the race, the sheer unreasonableness of the job, the circumnavigation of an entire country on a bicycle, village to village, along its shores, across its bridges, up and over the mountain peaks they call cols, requires a matchless stamina. The Tour is so taxing that Dutch rider Hennie Kuiper once said, after a long climb up an alp, "The snow had turned black in my eyes." It's not unlike the stamina of people who are ill every day. The Tour is a daily festival of human suffering, of minor tragedies and comedies, all conducted in the elements, sometimes terrible weather and sometimes fine, over flats, and into headwinds, with plenty of crashes. And it's three weeks long. Think about what you were doing three weeks ago. It feels like last year.

The race is very much like living—except that its consequences are less dire and there's a prize at the end. Life is not so neat.

There was no pat storybook ending for me. I survived cancer and made a successful comeback as a cyclist by winning the 1999 Tour, but that was more of a beginning than an end . . .

I've often said cancer was the best thing that ever happened to me.

Used by permission of Broadway Books, a division of Random House, Inc. From *Every Second Counts* by **Lance Armstrong** and Sally Jenkins, copyright © 2003 by Lance Armstrong.

__Lance Armstrong__ is a seven-time Tour de France racing cylcist winner and the recipient of numerous outstanding athlete and sportsman awards, *trophies, and accolades, including the 1999 ABC Wide World Athlete of the Year. He is the author of* It's Not About the Bike *and* My Journey Back to Life, *and is the founder of the Lance Armstrong Foundation which benefits cancer patients.* <u>*www.lancearmstrong.com*</u>

Orange Bowl "Warm-Up"

by Jim Rogers

The Colorado Buffaloes football team, as representatives of the Big Eight Conference, was on its way to the Orange Bowl for a playoff against the Clemson Tigers, the Atlantic Coast Conference champions, on New Year's Day, 1957.

We were eager and excited as we boarded our chartered plane and headed southeast, leaving the shivering cold of the Rocky Mountains behind. Not only were we looking forward to the thrill of possibly winning a bowl game, but to enjoying the many pleasurable perks that go along with it, especially some nice warm weather.

For starters, our team was being housed at the Bal Harbour Hotel, located in a luxurious upscale section of Miami. Then every two players were loaned a shiny new convertible to drive for the week. In addition, social events were being arranged in our honor, including a special dinner dance with the University of Miami coeds. To round it out, our training table was served top quality meals to keep us bulked-up in style.

Then there were the informal perks, so to speak, which involved "exploring" the nightlife in Miami. To do that, however, we had to sneak back into the hotel after curfew nearly every night. Although these events all occurred more than fifty years ago, three memorable stories still stand out, never to be forgotten.

First of all, my "convertible buddy," Wayne, and I went to a bar where we were warned by the bartender, "Be careful in here. There's a bunch of big burly guys over there and your lives won't be worth a plug nickel." We looked over to where he was gesturing, and darned if it wasn't a bunch of our very own teammates. We got a rousing chuckle out of that incident, plus it was a big boost to our football egos.

Another special memory involved Harry Belafonte, then a newly acclaimed singer whose calypso-type program we had enjoyed just the night before at the Fontainebleu Hotel in Miami Beach. We asked the hotel staff if we, as members of an Orange Bowl team, could somehow actually meet him. Sure enough, when they called his room, he gave the go-ahead for us to come on up. Belafonte was extremely welcoming to us, plus there were glamorous celebrity types and beautiful women up there, all of which made for an extremely enjoyable and entertaining evening.

Of course, we had to work hard at being inventive about evading the curfew each night. On one of the last nights, we were so late in returning to the hotel that only one room still had a light on. Once we arrived at our room, we realized the light was ours. With such daredevil behavior and our team's flamboyant lifestyle while in Miami—which made practices very tough—it's a wonder we weren't caught and suspended.

But on the night before the game itself, we noticed that they took no chances and housed us in the Marine barracks. Not much fun, but a good idea. The next day, we turned up so well rested that we won the Orange Bowl Classic 27-21!

__Jim Rogers__ is a seventy-four-year-old husband, father, and grandfather. After thirty-eight years, he retired from the computer industry where he worked on the Strategic Defense Initiative (SDI) Program for a major defense contractor. He remains active as an authorized IRS E-file provider, software developer, and part-time CTEC registered tax preparer.

My First Parachute Jump

by Mary Stage

The year was 1976, and I had decided the time had finally come for me to "jump" into the new sport I'd been dreaming about for years. "Jumping out of a perfectly good airplane . . ." was a common saying of "whofos," those of us who watched jumpers at the drop zone, but who never actually jumped.

Then, once I completed six hours of training and mustered up enough courage for the big moment, I wasn't even allowed to jump because the cloud ceiling was below 2500 feet. Two weeks later, however, after I'd gone through a refresher course in which I practiced 20 to 30 parachute landing falls known as PLFs, the intense moment came for me to actually board the Twin Beech skydiving aircraft. My heart was beating so fast, with adrenaline surging through every cell in my body, that I silently berated myself. Why on earth are you doing this?!! Why do something this scary?

Though I fully knew the procedure by heart, I could hardly believe my eyes when I looked down for a practice spot for my landing before jumping. The DZ (drop zone) appeared so tiny, with cars like ants and roads resembling zigzag ribbons. All the farms were plotted into 10—to 60-acre parcels and looked so neat. Once I caught myself staring at the ground, I realized I'd better follow my jumpmaster's directions to shut out further fear by totally concentrating and focusing on the job at hand.

I had heard about first-jump students who were so frozen with fear that they refused to jump and chose to ride the plane down instead. In the jump world, such a decision was considered a "no-no" because back in those days, most jump aircrafts were old, dilapidated rejects. So no one in their right mind wanted to land in a jump plane if they didn't have to.

I knew my parachute would open automatically because first-jumps were always static-lined, meaning that a nylon flat rope connected to an overhead metal bar in the plane would be attached to my backpack. Once I jumped out, the line would automatically pull open my backpack and a pilot chute would float out, inflate, and in turn, pull out my 28 double LL military orange and white round parachute. And in the event of a problem, I was equipped with a front-mounted reserve.

As I mentally reviewed these safety measures, my jumpmaster corrected my spot, and made certain I was in position. "Ready?" he shouted. "Go!" So out I tumbled and fall I did! Fortunately, the strict routine I was required to follow helped take my mind off the very real possibility of dying. Miraculously, I remembered to spread my arms out, thrust my neck back, make a huge arch, and count 1000, 2000, 3000. Then, thankfully, I felt the parachute inflate. Aaahh!

Very rapidly, I searched my parachute for holes, checked my lines for twists, and pulled on the brakes to test them for turning ability. Floating under my canopy felt peaceful, and my view of snow atop the local mountains was breathtakingly serene. Oh, how I wished I could prolong the thrill and inhale it forever, but soon realized it was already time to prepare for landing! So I looked for the windsock, calculated the wind direction, and faced it to slow my forward speed for a smoother landing. Other jumpers were gathered near the pea gravel—the target—shouting prompts, instructions, and reminding me to have feet and knees together, elbows tucked, and to prepare for a PLF. My landing was smooth and I felt proud.

Afterwards, I was filled with such exhilaration that I couldn't stop talking. I wanted to go right back up but knew I had to debrief first, then hear the critique on my jump. My jumpmaster congratulated me, offered a few suggestions, and said I was a "natural." I'll never forget his encouragement and inner knowledge that this would *not* be my first and only jump. For sure, I was hooked on a sport that would change my life for decades to come, including a long and happy marriage to a jump instructor who was both master and mentor to countless students.

As I look back on many more I-can't-believe-my-eyes experiences during my long, exhilarating jumping career, perhaps one of the most important to me ended up being the "Memorial Ash Dive" to honor the death of my dear husband, Bill Stage. Tradition calls for jumpers to celebrate a fellow jumper's death by spreading their ashes in the sky in memory of the dedication and formation of brotherhood that develops among followers of the sport. So at age sixty-three, several other "old timers" and I were privileged to spread Bill's ashes. It was then that I lovingly whispered to him, "Blue Skies," the traditional signature sign-off for a jumper.

Mary Stage *is a sixty-three-year-old retired teacher who enjoys writing about her teaching experiences, skydiving activities, and travels in the Pacific Northwest. Today, she works on her thirteen-acre parcel in Coarsegold, CA, with her Queensland heeler, Penny. sierraecho@sti.net*

Three Runs, One Hit, and Two Errors

by Alan Rosenbluth

To my own astonishment, I returned to playing softball at age sixty-eight. Over the years, I was frequently mistaken for other white-headed guys.

I recall one time in Austin, Texas—three months before my thirtieth birthday—when I was playing shortstop in an over-thirty softball league. My age was calculated by rounding up to thirty years. But more importantly, I wasn't asked my age or for any confirming documents. One night, I happened to play a very extraordinary game. On a crucial play with two outs and bases loaded, I dove for a grounder up the middle and the ball lodged in my glove's webbing. While still on my knees, I backhanded it to the second baseman for the out.

Next inning, a good jump on the blooper down the third base line allowed me to reach a ball outside the range of three fielders, with another diving one-handed catch. Then at bat with two on base, and noting that the opposing short fielder was in the gap in left center, I wanted to hit to right. The pitch was high and outside, and I stroked it. The ball tracked well over the second baseman's extended glove.

Well, it rocketed along the parched dirt between two outfielders, a sure triple! The right fielder got it as I rounded second base. Then our team captain, Mike Rodell, made a bad call. His left arm wind milled toward home plate, giving me the "go" sign. I knew he was wrong, and I'd be an easy out. But the old discipline resurfaced. You follow the base coach's decision even if it's obtuse, as it was this time. Rounding third, I knew it was hopeless. Indeed, the catcher had the ball with me still ten feet away. Smiling, he blocked the plate with one knee and prepared to tag me sliding through the dirt. Again, without thought, I yielded to my training. Not sliding, I dropped my shoulder and hit him full speed with a chest-high forearm shiver. He collapsed, cap flying, mitt and ball rolling in opposite directions. Hitting the catcher high, my momentum carried me right through him into a front flip, landing flat on my back in billowing dust. A home run.

Why wasn't I happy? I'd followed the coach's judgment as I'd been taught. But this wasn't the World Series, or even an important high school game, where I certainly would have tried with everything I had. I knew it wasn't right to hit an aging catcher that way, that hard, in a meaningless game in Texas. From within my spinning head, I heard my father say, "I never taught you to play like that."

Apologizing to the catcher, I remained angry with Mike Rodell for sending me around. I was even more dissatisfied with myself. Achieve something if possible, but don't think you're good when you defeat someone with unnecessary harshness.

Obviously, my emotions took control of this story. What I intended to convey was that I played softball unusually well one night decades ago. At game's end, the other team's captain insisted I was too young for this league. He said I was nowhere near thirty years old, thrust out his chin, and awaited my response. An overdue particle of better judgment sealed my lips. Rather, I looked down and pulled off my dirty baseball cap. His mouth made a large *O*, and I could see more than one gold tooth. Eyes widening, he noticed that my hair was nearly 50 percent white and belonged to a sweaty, dirty man of probably more than forty years. Mumbling inaudibly, the perplexed team captain plodded away, shaking his head sadly.

On that remarkable night, I was for the first and only time mistaken for someone significantly younger *and* significantly older than I really was at the time. And the same guy made both errors.

Alan Rosenbluth *is a retired pharmacy professor and dean who enjoys senior softball, yoga, tai chi, Rotary, and Lifelong Learning. He and wife, Gwen, live in Morgantown, West Virginia. He has published several short fiction and memoir pieces.* rosenbluthg@aol.com

Ole's Hakai Pass

by Martha Scott

I've never been a "fisherperson," but I sure got hooked during a week at Ole's Fishing Lodge, north of Vancouver, British Columbia. First, the Grumman Goose—our eight-seat commuter plane—roared our family over a jigsaw puzzle of rocky islands covered with lush spruce and hemlock. Once its pontoons skidded to an exciting wet stop on Hakai Pass, we were motored to the floating fishing lodge, which was perched on a barge and tucked in a cove away from all wind and currents in the pass. And so began our wonderful, wild week of memorable fishing in the beautiful remote Canadian wilderness. Each day was spectacular in its own special way, right up to the last minute.

Then I recall how, on the last night of our stay, a nearby boat radioed us an alert of lots of dolphin activity in the area. The low sun angle caused a golden glow above the glassy waters. As dying winds magnified the haunting calls of circling birds, their white feathers lit up like neon lights against the dark rain forest. As we motored forward, we realized that the waters were filled with thousands of fish churning just beneath the surface.

As we grew closer, we were fascinated by airborne dolphins seemingly swept up in a confusion of activity. Pods of dolphins resembled bucking broncos as they galloped in all directions. Some zigzagged by us, shooting up spray that sizzled in their wakes. Others thrilled us as they leaped right in front of our boat while I groped for my camera. Then under the transom darted little bullet bodies, jet propelled and screaming like torpedoes.

A sudden massive exhale blast across the cove from two young humpback whales at the center of this feeding frenzy surprised us. First there was silence, followed by an explosive vertical spray from cavernous lungs as the whales scooped up fish with oversized flippers, then dove with their tail flukes waving. Still soaring overhead were birds all lit up in an aerial dance, swooping to the dark sky, then plunging into the inky waters.

As the sun angle lowered, the dolphins turned west, slippery bodies frolicking into the currents of Hakai Pass and the ocean beyond. The energy subsided; the whales were hiding in the depths. We motored towards the glowing horizon for a time, not saying a word, longing, wishing we could see more of these amazing, captivating gray-suited travelers.

"Yellow Mellow," our skiff, turned back and mechanically grumbled home. No one wanted to break the magic spell with words. Birds still rocked on the quieting waters, and the silent evergreens dripped in the rain forest all around. Gazing back over the pass and hoping for a last squinting glimpse of the traveler, we enjoyed the gift of an exclamation point rainbow with a delicate spectrum of colors glowing against the dark forest. Incredulous, we watched the luminous ribbon drift gently, silently, directly over the cove where nature had given us its show. The floating colors were hanging there in the mist, marking that most alive place. "Hello," the colors breathed, revealing themselves from the void. The vision lasted for a heartbeat and a whisper.

None of us spoke, but our wide eyes glistened and our grateful hearts thumped a deep internal thank you. This meeting with the wild felt like a divine gift, a cosmic door opening just a crack for a surprise look into the beautiful and the powerfully loving realm of "The Mystery." "Who are you?" I asked the rainbow. We felt the silent response.

The following morning, we had until 10:00 a.m. to catch "The Big One." I caught a seventeen-pound salmon, and a treasured picture proves it. But it's the glimpse into that other wild and free world that

I will cherish and honor the most. I know I'm hooked. Such a sacred, shimmering memory will feed me long after the big coho salmon's sweet pink meat has all been eaten.

Martha Scott *is a sixty-six-year-old retired school teacher and "non-fisherperson" who just loves any excuse to be immersed in the breathtaking beauty and enjoyment of nature.*

Special Moments

by Carol Mann

ecember 1944; Williamsville, New York. There I was, clumping along behind my father, trying to ice skate, hating my blue snowsuit and bulky leggings. I wanted beautiful flesh-colored tights and a glamorous short skirt like Sonja Henie wore. Father skated ahead with long, graceful strides, his hands clasped behind him, and the shiny blades on his black skates glinting in the daylight. A 1930s-style tweed cap shaded his eyes; a plaid jacket warmed him.

Suddenly, I stopped. There was a crack in the ice, right in front of me! *Step on a crack, break your mother's back!* I *never* step on a crack, so why would I ever want to skate over one? The crack snaked across the ice like a huge python seen on the pages of a *National Geographic* magazine. Why did father bring me here to Ellicott Creek Park? Why not skate closer to home? But he just glided back and forth, away from the crack and me.

"Come on, Carol," he pressed.

"There's a great big crack here!" My voice was high-pitched and thin.

"Just skate over it. I want to show you something," he said calmly, brushing me off.

Three skaters glided over the chasm, but I couldn't move. Father motioned me forward. Did he really have something to show me or was it a trick to make me go over the crack? Stiff-legged, I pushed closer. The blades on my new white figure skates cut tiny gashes in the ice. My mouth felt dry.

I peeked into the crack, quickly looking away. Thick, thick ice. My third grade teacher had just explained, "During the Ice Age, glaciers crept across the earth. Perhaps it was the reason dinosaurs became extinct." Could dinosaurs and glaciers be *this* close? What if a dinosaur survived beneath the surface, ready to pull me into the icy water? I couldn't breathe.

"Let's go, Carol." Father's voice was now becoming crisper to hurry me.

Time with my father was precious. I had to show, to prove, I wasn't afraid. He'd think I was a big baby. I put the toe of my right skate behind me. The blade's jagged teeth snagged the ice. My heart beat faster, my eyes squeezed shut, I managed to shove off, launched on one leg.

"Good!" shouted a voice inside my head. "Push your legs to go faster, pump the air with your arms." I felt a bump. The crack! *Push! Push!* an inner forced urged. *Skate! Skate!* I didn't know I could go so fast. *Skate! Skate*! I opened my eyes. A quick glance behind revealed no monster, no monster at all, only a stupid sissy crack.

Father waited. Taking my hand, he skated beside me, showing me how to match my strides to his. We skated in a figure eight and then continued up the creek. Push, glide, push, glide. I watched my wobbly ankles wobble less. Father then put his hand out to stop me. "This is what I wanted you to see."

"Oh, I didn't know they could . . ."

"Sh-h-h-h, listen," he whispered.

Before us hung Ellicott Creek Falls. Majestic. Frozen. A silent wall of cascading aqua blue ice draped with snow. We didn't move. Father squeezed my hand as white powdered snow fell gently around us. It settled on our eyelashes, like tears. Now I was grateful that only minutes ago I had managed to summon my courage and conquer my fear.

Carol Mann, seventy-four, is a retired educator-turned-writer whose work has been published in both literary journals and magazines. She currently serves on the board of directors of the National League of American Pen Women, Palm Springs, California Branch. cstanfield@dc.rr.com

Chapter 7:
SPIT, FEATHERS, & OTHER HUMOROUS PHILOSOPHIES

The Many Uses of Spit

by Shirley Huston

The word "spit" arouses slightly sordid or distasteful imagery, wouldn't you say? And yet, isn't our saliva—more colloquially called *spit*—a very useful accessory that helps us meet many ordinary daily needs? Think about it. Don't we all use spit in one way or another without giving it a second thought, even when others are watching? Consider the following many uses of spit:

To moisten the tip of a thread so it glides through the eye of a needle.

To lick the thumb and forefinger before struggling to open one of those stubborn plastic bags after tearing it from a roll in the fruit and vegetable department.

To smooth an eyebrow, wipe a spot of dust from your shoe, or wipe a smudge from just about anything you find smudged.

To wet your thumb before counting money or thumbing through pages of the telephone book.

To make a child's cowlick stay down during a photo session.

To moisten your fingertip before picking up the last crumb from that delicious dessert while no one else is looking.

To test for wind direction . . . but then everyone knows that!

Shirley Huston is a retired marketing executive who "unretired" in order to serve as executive director of a trade association for thirteen years. She has written a newspaper column, as well as numerous media and corporate promotional materials. Shirley is a literary agent and editor for several budding authors. shuston.litagent@verizon.net

Grouch Prevention 101

by Melody Fleming

Everyone is in such a hurry and so stressed out these days. The world has become a frightening place. Consequently, the need for laughter in our lives has never been greater than it is today. Laughing matters because it is a natural stress reliever, and even in small doses, laughter can give us hope for the future. Laughter is one of the simplest and most basic ways to enliven our lives and connect with others. In spite of that, most of us don't laugh enough!

Often we equate growing up with becoming serious. At some point you may have come to believe that in order to be mature, you must stifle your silliness. WRONG! If you are too busy to laugh, then you are entirely too busy. If you don't get your daily dose of laughter, you are at high risk of developing hardening of the attitudes and becoming a grouch!

GROUCH POTENTIAL QUIZ

1. Do you frequently commiserate with others on the state of the world today, rehashing the old "going to hell in a hand-basket" routine?
2. Has your get-up-and-go, got-up-and-went?
3. Do you spend more time remembering the good ol' days instead of enjoying the present?
4. Has it been awhile since you've tried something new and adventurous?
5. Do you frequently find yourself discussing your aches and pains?

6. Do you frequently say "Good grief, it's morning," instead of "Good morning"?
7. Do you seem to be having more bad days than good?

If you answered "yes" to any of these questions, you may be suffering from: N.L.E. (Not Laughing Enough) and could possibly even have Grouch potential, an infectious disease. This can occur at any age, so it might be wise to take a "check-up from the neck-up." Being a grouch is no way to run your life.

If you are upbeat and positive, you are like a people-magnet at any age, but if you are negative and grouchy, it's not really good for us to be around you. Remember, it's never too late to change your habits, perspectives, and attitudes in order to bring more laughter and joy into your life. The choice is yours. Do you choose "grouch" or "glee"?

BEGIN WITH A SMILE

When you're happy and in a good mood, it's easy to smile, but what about those days when you're in a funk? If you just don't feel like smiling, then fake it. Yes, fake it! Your body does not know it is a phony smile. Your zygomaticus (smile muscles) are linked to your thymus gland, so whether your smile is genuine or fake, you are still getting the benefit of strengthening the thymus gland, an important contributor to a healthy immune system. Chances are, the person you gave the fake smile to will give a genuine one in return. This gives you a little dose of their life energy, which improves your mood, making your next smile heartfelt. Smiling gives both psychological and physical benefits. A smile is a precursor to a laugh. Smiling, like laughing, is contagious. If you want to bring more laughter into your life, start with a smile. Remember, winners are grinners!

CREATE YOUR OWN LAUGHTER THERAPY PLAN

Just as your body needs a regularly scheduled exercise plan, you also need a laughter plan. What makes me laugh may not make you laugh. That's why you'll need a unique plan of your own. Here are some suggestions you might incorporate into your laughter plan:

1. **Hang out with friends who make you laugh**. If you are living with a spouse who is a grouch, there's not much you can do about it. (Grouch prevention is an inside job.) The good news is you can choose your friends. Try to spend as much time as possible with positive, fun people.

2. **Learn to laugh at yourself and you will be constantly entertained**. Instead of getting upset with your mistakes and listening to your negative self-talk . . . stop! Learn from your mistakes and then laugh at them. Admit to yourself, at times, that you are downright "goofy."

3. **Look for the funny.** Try changing your perspective as to how you view everyday occurrences. The way we see things is what we believe, and what we believe is our reality, whether it's true or not. Our beliefs filter all the information we receive. If we believe life is hard and humorless, our belief filter will only give us this type of information. Likewise, if we believe life abounds with humor, our belief filter will show us just how funny life really is.

4. **Start your very own funny file.** Collect jokes, cartoons, funny sayings, and articles that make you laugh. Keep them handy to share with friends or to review when you're feeling a little down.

5. **Make time in your day to do something silly**. Dance a little jig, make a funny face, or sing a silly song. If you make one person a day laugh, in one year you will have made a whole village happy.

6. **Smile more**. This sets the tone for positive emotions.

7. **Make a list of the things you absolutely love to do, and make sure you do them**. The only difference between a rut and a grave is the depth. Go for the gusto . . . Live juicy! Enthusiasm makes us come alive.

8. **Immerse yourself whenever possible in humor.** Know what tickles your funny bone. Some people like slapstick, while others prefer a more intellectual type of humor. Once you know your preference, go look for your favorites: stand-up comics, good sitcoms, or humorous videos and books.

9. **Play more**. Get into your child-self. Play with your kids, grandkids, or pets. Play games: Balderdash, Cranium, etc. Play harmless tricks on coworkers, friends, and family. They'll love it.

10. **Make a mental list of the funniest moments in your life.** Then call one to mind when you are feeling stressed. The good feeling that the memory evokes in your body may momentarily relieve tension, just long enough for you to get a different perspective on the situation at hand.

11. **Get yourself some "prop power."** Start a collection of humorous props: clown noses, Billy Bob Teeth, weird glasses, whoopee whistles, crazy hats, talking toys, rubber chickens, etc. Chances are the items that make you laugh will make your friends laugh too.

12. **Share embarrassing moments with a friend.** This creates a closeness that allows us to see one another as we really are: imperfect, stumbling, bumbling humor beings.

13. **Relive your childhood.** Have a pillow fight, jump on the bed, blow bubbles, fly a kite, tell spooky stories and scream.

14. **Celebrate often, for any reason.** How about a reincarnation party, where everyone comes as they were? Have a couch potato football fete, or a sci-fi spree. Figure out creative ways to have fun and laugh.

15. **Find something wonderful each day to be grateful for.** Laughter has a magical power of its own and is a wonderful stress-buster, so keep inviting it into your life as much as possible!

Melody Fleming *is a newspaper columnist, speaker, and author* of Laffing Matters—A Grouch Prevention Handbook. *She is a retired junior and senior high school teacher who has also taught at the university level. Melody is a certified laughter leader (CLL) and longtime member of Association for Applied and Therapeutic Humor, as well as the National League of American Pen Women.* www.laffing-matters.com

Laughter

by Maria Shriver

I've asked myself where I learned to be both so ambitious and driven on the one hand, and so willing to laugh at myself on the other. It think I've figured it out. My mother.

My mother made it very clear to me that it was a man's world, and it was no use complaining about it. From the time I was little, she pushed me to do whatever my brothers did. "Just get in there, Maria. Get in there and do it." If it was a boys-only football game, she made sure I played, no matter how disgusted they were at the prospect. But really it was up to me to participate. "Get in there, Maria. Get in there and play," she pushed me. And I'd shove my way in. For a long time my brothers wouldn't throw the football to me . . .

After what seemed like several years of football games, they finally threw the ball to me and tackled me. At last! It wasn't all that different from when they'd pile on and tickle me to distraction, but I was playing football! I was so bad at the game compared to them, I had to laugh at myself. They certainly did. And I grew up with that voice in my ear—"Get in there, Maria. Just get in there and do it!"—and also the sound of laughter, me laughing at my own nerve. The lesson I learned was to take what I *do* seriously, but not take *myself* so seriously.

I did something last year. I felt I was missing the fun I'd experienced in my twenties and figured I needed an attitude adjustment. So I sat down and asked myself what I did back then that made me so happy. What made me laugh? To be honest, some of the things I couldn't do again, and I won't get into what those were. But I remembered what a great time I used to have playing sports. So I've started playing tennis and biking with my kids. And I remembered how much I laughed when I spent time with my brothers and my cousins. So I've made a point to schedule family vacation time every summer with them back East where I grew up. That week of laughter feeds my soul all year long.

And instead of blowing off my high school reunion, I went to it and laughed at memories with old girlfriends . . . I find when I have an accurate picture of myself—and accept and appreciate where I am in my life and where I still want to go—that's when I have the perspective and attitude that allows me to enjoy myself and have a good laugh.

The love and the laughter are what you need most in your life. They'll fill out all the potholes in the road.

Reprinted by permission of Grand Central Publishing. From *Ten Things I Wish I'd Known—Before I Went Out into the Real World* by **Maria Shriver**. Copyright © 2000 by Maria Shriver.

Maria Shriver was an NBC News co-anchor and winner of a Peabody Award. She is a journalist, author of six books, a former First Lady of California, and a member of the John F. Kennedy family. www.mariashriver.com

An Evening at the Chicken Ranch Brothel

by Jeanne Greene

It was time to begin planning the 1982 three-day regional convention of the Southern Nevada Chapter of Mensa. Joyce Rogers-Rooker and I were the appointed cochairs of the event,

So first, she and I reserved the Imperial Palace Hotel, made arrangements for the Saturday banquet, then discussed plans to distribute hospitality bags of casino trinkets such as key chains, dice, cards, pens, etc. It was then that Joyce came up with a very amusing idea. To add a touch of fun to the bag—plus a little unique local color—why not also include something from the Chicken Ranch? It could be a "Ladies-Your-Way" menu, book of matches, or even a postcard.

This world-famous Chicken Ranch Brothel is located about sixty miles from Las Vegas in Pahrump, Nevada, in Nye County, where prostitution and brothels are legal. The license is actually considered the most privileged license in the state of Nevada. We knew that the ranch had recently been sold to Russ Reade, a tenured high school biology teacher, and businessman Kenneth Green, both from San Francisco.

So we decided to place a call to the ranch, and to our surprise, our call was immediately directed straight to Russ. Russ politely explained that he'd be unable to donate souvenirs to us at that time because the brothel was undergoing a facelift and that menus and souvenirs were also being revamped. However, he offered to make it up to us with the following proposal. Once the remodel was completed, he'd invite us—plus five or six other Mensa women of our choosing—to have dinner at the ranch and spend the evening chatting with the ladies.

Well, we didn't hesitate a minute, and happily accepted his apology and kind invitation!

When the appointed date finally arrived, we invited Mensa members Rochelle, Becky, C.C., Ann, and June to join us for this special evening. Russ had cautioned us in advance that there'd be only one rule we'd be asked to follow. We'd be permitted to ask the ladies whatever we were curious about, *except* for one thing. We were not to ask them anything about the money they earned. He also wanted permission to tell the girls that they could ask *us* anything, too. We said absolutely.

So on this special night, the seven of us dressed in casual clothes, jeans, T-shirts, skirts, and blouses. We had purchased an appropriate gift for the ladies and, with that in hand, off we all went. The brothel is situated on forty acres of land and boasts its own landing strip. There are seventeen bedrooms, plus three extensively decorated theme bungalows that cater to customers seeking a more luxurious experience. Upon arrival, we were greeted by ten very lovely ladies, all dressed in sleek evening gowns or filmy lingerie. Their hair and makeup were done to perfection and they ranged in age from eighteen to thirty-five. First, we were given a tour of a few of the bedrooms, then of the theme bungalows, Leghorn Bar, kitchen, and dining room.

Although the working girls were not permitted to have alcohol, we were offered any drink of our choice. So for over one hour, our conversation went back and forth with an exchange of questions, answers, and personal stories. Everyone was definitely having a great time! We found them to be intelligent, and they found us to be open-minded and not at all judgmental.

The ladies freely shared stories about how they got into the business. Some had children living with relatives, others had college degrees, and one had a master's degree. Their work schedule consisted of twenty-one days at the ranch, then seven days away from the property. One woman—the oldest lady in the group—shared some very personal information. She told us that she was married and lived with her husband in Texas. On her seven-day rotation, she'd return home to Texas to spend a week with her husband. The only financial information we were privy to was that this same lady earned more money than anyone else in the house!

We, in turn, shared details about our own lives back in Las Vegas—how we made our living and where we worked. Four of us were single and three were married. Did we have children? Yes, a total of nine.

Then, in came the cook to announce that dinner was served. We were delightfully surprised as we sat down to a beautiful meal of elegance, consisting of filet mignon, baked potato, asparagus, Caesar salad, plus a selection of desserts. Following dinner, as we were continuing our enjoyable conversations with the ladies of the ranch, the doorbell rang at 8:00 p.m. The madam went to answer it, then ushered in a young man about twenty-three years old who seemed totally unprepared for what was to happen next.

Russ quickly asked if we seven would like to be included in the lineup. Knowing full well that we were safe from being selected, yet nevertheless feeling nervous, we answered, "Sure." We lined up, interspersed between the "girls," and—wouldn't you know it—the gentleman picked Rochelle.

At that point, Russ was forced to step in and explain that we weren't really "working girls," but guests of the ranch, and asked if he'd please pick another girl. Afterwards, we all laughed and had a fun time teasing Rochelle. Then Rochelle, being Jewish, was affectionately dubbed the "Chosen One." We still call her that to this day.

It was nearly 11:00 p.m. when we thanked all the ladies for being so open and gracious to us and for showing us such a great time. The ladies, in turn, thanked each of us, then presented Rochelle with a Chicken Ranch T-shirt that read, "I was laid at the Chicken Ranch."

Scribbled in indelible ink, however, they had cleverly inserted the word "almost," and had it signed by Russ, the girls, and also the young man. We, in turn, gave them the gift we had brought, a brass wall plaque engraved with the following words: "Quality is Remembered Long after the Price is Forgotten."—Gucci Family Motto

It was an evening none of us will ever forget!

Footnote: Russ Reade remains a friend of the Southern Nevada Mensa Group and often speaks at our regional gatherings. He's been an instrumental force in the reform and cleanup of the brothel industry by having legislation passed requiring frequent medical examinations of all working girls. Besides which, he offers continuing education courses in finance, drug and alcohol abuse, planning for retirement, and high school GED curriculum to all of his female employees.

Jeanne Greene *is a seventy-three-year-old retired business manager and accountant who has written a narrative of the first forty years of her life. Writing has become her passion. She is an active grandmother who lives on two beautiful acres in the foothills of Yosemite National Park, and enjoys her longtime relationship with Rod.* meanjean@sierratel.com *or (559) 977-4433*

Ms. Malaprop

by Gordon W. Fredrickson

During my very first parent-teacher conferences a parent hinted at the type of play I should direct.

"We should be able to understand it," she said.

"OK," I said with interest.

"It should be funny, not serious. I like real funny plays."

"Something farcical?" I suggested.

"What?"

"You know, a farce."

"Shame on you!" she exclaimed and abruptly left the room.

From *Stories Teachers Tell* with permission of author **Gordon W. Fredrickson**, copyright owner.

Gordon is a retired English teacher, play director, and farmer. His goal is to preserve the heritage of the small farms in Minnesota by writing stories about a farm family, set in 1950, which are then performed in schools, museums, libraries, and other organizations. www.gordonfredrickson. com

Deer Camp

by Nancy C. Lydick

The spirit of adventure must surely be lacking in my brain. I have known my husband, Edward, for nearly fifty years and whenever deer season approaches, he reminds me of a four-year-old who can't wait for Christmas. I have never understood what makes it so exciting for him and his buddies to go to their favorite cabin in the boonies, where for years they didn't even have an indoor bathroom and were forced to bathe in the river. In November and December! Even in Arkansas, that's a bit too cold for the not-so-faint-of-heart.

The cabin is furnished with give-away donations or homemade furniture, including appliances that were clearly headed for the trash. Over time, it became a neighborhood joke: "Don't throw it away; I'll take it to Deer Camp."

Getting up before dawn is not my idea of fun, but it's what they do. And while these "great hunters" are deep in the woods, they contend with wasps, chiggers, ticks, spiders, rattlesnakes, water moccasins, and wild pigs. They cheerfully pay good money to put up with all this. After all, they have a cabin in which to sleep, complete with little critters of its own that only come out in the dark of night.

But I do feel good about one thing. It seems to me that anyone who can spend three, four, or maybe five weeks a year in this cabin can surely overlook a little dust and dog hair at home.

Yes, I certainly must be lacking some gene that keeps me from doing all those things in the spirit of adventure, and will always wish I knew who to thank for that.

Nancy C. Lydick *is a eighty-nine-year-old happily married housewife and mother of five sons who lives with her husband and two spoiled dogs in Bryant, Arkansas. She enjoys writing, playing pool, and attending senior dances with her husband. 1420 Pleasant Pointe Circle, Bryant, AR 72011*

The Living End

by Andrea Giambrone

Maybe it's me. Maybe we all do it. In my case, it started years ago when I saw this quote: "No one ever said, 'I should have worked more' on their tombstone."

I spotted it near the door as I was rushing out of a Beverly Hills restaurant, late for my next meeting. It stopped me cold in my tracks. I guess you could call it a *BOING* moment. I was working like a demon, logging in lots of hours, with the stress to show for it. Young though I was, it made me stop and think about the kind of life I really wanted to live.

Perhaps because of that tombstone reminder, I've come to have a special appreciation for epitaphs. No, it isn't morbidity. For one thing, it's my lifelong fascination with words.

I've been anywhere from touched to tickled with the more inventive tombstones I've seen. After all, attending funerals is an unavoidable part of living, although that didn't stop Woody Allen from commenting, "I don't want to achieve immortality through my work; I want to achieve it by not dying."

He would appreciate how having the "last say" can actually be laugh-inducing. It sure says a lot more about the person than a generic "Dearly departed."

You just might enjoy a few of the epitaphs I've unearthed (so to speak). They happen to be real ones, dating anywhere from the eighteenth century to last month.

For a dentist: "John Brown is filling his last cavity."

The epitaph written and used for himself by Sir Winston Churchill: "I am ready to meet my Maker. Whether my Maker is prepared for the great ordeal of meeting me is another matter."

I'd say read 'em and weep, but it's certainly more appropriate to suggest that you read 'em and laugh!

"Here lies John Yeast. Pardon me for not rising."

"She loved opera and she hated ironing."

"She drank good ale, good punch and wine, and lived to the age of ninety-nine."

"Here lies an atheist. All dressed up and no place to go."

"The buck stopped here."

On an attorney's tombstone, "The defense rests."

And this gem of ingenuity, "I told you I was sick."

My all-time favorite was spoken by Dustin Hoffman during a *Sixty Minutes* interview. When the interviewer asked the famous actor if he'd ever thought about what he would want on his tombstone, Hoffman reflected for a bit. Soon, a mischievous smile crossed his face, and he said, "Yeah, what I want written is, 'I knew this would happen.'"

I only hope I can be as clever when it comes to having the last word about myself. Since one of the columns I've written over the years was titled, "Ya Gotta Laugh," I thought about using that. But I decided it might lack the necessary, dare I say "depth," that I would like associated with my demise. Unless, of course, I meet my end with a large martini in one hand in the midst of telling the funniest story I know.

In which case, what do you think about "The Last Laugh"? Or, since a Shakespearean quote would certainly pay homage to one of the greatest writers of all time, I might have to give serious consideration to, "All's well that ends well."

Andrea Giambrone has had a lifelong love affair with writing, and is a professional speaker, columnist, advertising writer, and published poet. As a freelance consultant and president of her own advertising service, Think a la Carte, *Andrea is the supreme and consummate wordsmith.* www.thinkalacarte.com *or* ag@thinkalacarte.com

Just Call Me Emeril

by Gloria Burke

Many cities are so overrun with restaurants these days, and my Midwestern hometown is certainly no exception. But I'm proud to say that I am a devotee of fine dining, be it filet mignon at a pricey steakhouse or a burger broiled to juicy perfection at Burger King.

It's not that I don't enjoy cooking. In fact, in my younger days, I always loved showcasing my culinary skills (I'd like to believe I could easily have been mistaken for a female Emeril Lagasse). It was nothing for me to spend days preparing for an upcoming dinner party in my home. In those days, I considered someone's request for one of my recipes the greatest compliment I could ever receive. Back in the fifties and sixties, my husband and I loved to entertain as many as twelve dinner guests at a time at a sit-down dinner party. For me, it was great fun creating a menu that was guaranteed to please. My Eastlake dining room table, circa 1900, could seat twelve comfortably, and a smaller group of six would fit just as nicely with a few leaves removed.

Once the house had been preened, polished, and fluffed to what I considered "guest status," I was ready to face the "dinner party challenge." The huge *not*-permanent-press Irish linen tablecloth and matching napkins were ironed to slippery-smooth perfection several days in advance, with the table dressed and decorated the night before to ensure that no minor detail was overlooked. My mother's delicate 1918 Minton antique fine china and elegant sterling silver service made exquisite table setting accents.

Would I do it now? Absolutely not. With each passing year, it became more like work and today it's hard for me to even believe that I once loved all that elaborate menu planning, shopping at various grocery stores in search of the *exact* right ingredients at the *exact* right price, hauling it home, storing, preparing, and serving it on the day of the event. No dinner party could happen in the '50s or '60s without lots of loose ends remaining for the big day itself. Even with all my meticulous, careful, exact advance planning, on more than one occasion, I recall cutting it right down to the wire, still rushing about as the guests were ringing the doorbell.

I'd be willing to bet that most women under forty today couldn't even imagine preparing dinner for twelve without having the help of a dishwasher or microwave. Meat, especially beef, had to be browned first, then seasoned and baked at just the right temperature until it reached that delectable, mouth-watering stage. Real potatoes had to be peeled, boiled, and mashed so they would be the perfect consistency when the dinner guests sat down at the table. Vegetables were cooked on top of the stove and timed so they wouldn't come out mushy and soft.

Today, "Let's eat out" is my mantra. I confess yielding and succumbing to the "restaurant call" whether I'm alone or with others. So where did the "I-love-cooking" girl go? I think she's left the kitchen today for easier, more carefree pastures.

Gloria Burke ~ *It wasn't until Gloria began teaching a "Writing Your Memories" class for adults in 1992 that her own writing career took off. She has taught English classes at the middle, high school and college levels for many years. At eighty-three, she still works. (419) 885-1413*

Lucille Ball

by Paul Ryan

I worked with Lucille Ball at the end of her career on the 1989 Academy Awards show. She was a presenter, and I was coaching some of the presenters. She was a serious person in real life, and had a very low voice from her years of smoking. I played backgammon with her—trust me, she was a very serious player.

Lucy had been a B-actress in dramatic movies, and was as surprised as anyone else when she became a hot commodity in comedy. It just goes to show that you never know when comedy genius is going to hit! Lucy was an experimental comedienne, willing to make a fool of herself at the drop of a hat. Her genius at physical comedy is rare, and will be honored forever. It was an honor to be in the same room with her; she will make us laugh for a very long time.

Use Lucy as a prime example of someone whose comedy brilliance didn't shine until she met the right person to complement it, which was—of course—Desi Arnaz.

Reprinted from The Art of Comedy: Getting Serious About Being Funny, *with permission of author* **Paul Ryan***, renowned Hollywood comedy acting and TV hosting/media coach; on the Emmy ballot as Bruce on "Desperate Housewives"; "Entertainment Tonight" correspondent; series co-host of "Mid-Morning L.A."; host/ producer of 175 shows for the Travel Channel and "The Paul Ryan Show." www. paulryanproductions.com*

Shy Suitor

by Mary Jane Rollheiser

Billy, a senior man in his seventies, once surprised me by bringing me a bouquet of "nearly dead" flowers at the bank window where I worked as a teller. Of course, I thanked him politely and told him it was very nice of him to be so thoughtful. I noticed he acted very shy. Then from that time on, he always waited patiently in line so he could approach my window. Again and again, he continued to bring me gifts of old fruit or candy. Again and again, I said thank you.

But one day when he came up to my window, quite unexpectedly, he blurted out, "I need to throw you in the back seat of my car with a six-pack and take you out to Palm Springs!"

I was so taken back by his unexpected forcefulness that I said that my husband might not like that.

"I don't care," he answered. "Where does he work?"

Somewhat puzzled, and of course slightly caught off guard, I told him what he wanted to know. My husband was already aware of Billy anyway, and said he'd wait for him to come into his workplace.

The following week, Billy really did go visit my husband, who knew what he looked like and was ready and expecting him. Billy walked straight up to him and declared, "Well, I was going to marry her first!" Then he suddenly turned around and left as abruptly as he had arrived.

So from that day on, all the girls at the bank could hardly wait to see what was going to happen to me next. Years later, I myself am now a senior and loving it, although I do enjoy reflecting on the many happy years when I worked with lots of wonderful, and occasionally colorful, customers.

And I'll admit, I miss Billy; in fact, I still have many good laughs just thinking about him.

Mary Jane Rollheiser, *sixty-six, retired after a long career in the banking industry. She loves to cook, read, garden, attend car shows, and is very proud of the 1972 Nova she restored. She also has fun boating at her river house.*

Fountain of Youth

by Alan Rosenbluth

I've been retired from work for four years now and enjoy being casual. I can sleep late. No neckties. Mostly jeans, khakis, tee shirts, sweat shirts. Running shoes, even when not running. Stuff like that. One favorite luxury is not shaving for a day, or two, or three . . .

My wife, Gwen, was happy for me most of the time, but one day she said, "You really should shave today before we leave the house. You look so much better." I didn't even look up from my book, so she cleverly supplied the kicker. "You look ten years younger when you shave," she whispered in my ear.

Fifteen minutes later, as we left the house, my face was as smooth as the proverbial baby's bottom. Neither Gwen nor I addressed the topic again. And yet, I've remembered her words every day while removing dangerous bristles that unfairly accelerate the aging process. Finally the implications struck me fully in the face. If shaving once removes ten years from my appearance, then shaving twice would set my time clock back twenty years.

Gwen doesn't know it, but I recently began shaving twice a day.

And last week, a new routine emerged. I now put razor to face before each meal and at bedtime. Since the process has developed gradually over time, Gwen still hasn't realized that I'm looking forty years younger than I did a few months back. But it's obvious to me that a thirty-one-year-old kid now shares my bathroom mirror. That's a good bit younger than our sons, Kirby and Brady. Wow!

Last week, the new West Virginia University football coach nodded to me as I walked near the campus. I could tell he wanted to ask if I had any eligibility left. But the poor guy was just too shy to inquire. In the future, I'll try to make him more comfortable so he can speak freely.

As images of my upcoming college and professional athletic careers come to mind, the logical next step, of course, is endorsements—that's where the real money is. Naturally, my business agent will recruit people from Gillette, Norelco, Colgate, Remington, and others to bid on my services. Think of me on TV, suggesting to an aging audience that shaving is scientifically proven to trim ten years off their appearance, and that the effect can be further multiplied by repeating the treatment. I predict the razor industry will explode!

We know that many citizens will not stop at shaving two times. After all, look what it's done for me. You'll soon see me sell this concept not only on TV, but also on radio, via direct mailings, and the internet. Michael Jordan, Warren Buffett, and Anna Kournikova will surely invite me to join their private investment club.

Soon, I'll be attending my class reunion. Back in 1951, we graduated from McAlester High School together. Who would have thought that one of us would become a multibillionaire? They'll be so proud of me.

Alan Rosenbluth *is a retired pharmacy professor and dean who enjoys senior softball, yoga, tai chi, and Lifelong Learning. He and wife, Gwen, live in Morgantown, West Virginia. He has published several short fiction and memoir pieces.*

We Are the Young

by Phyllis Costello

When I was a small child, nearly everyone around me seemed old. Being so young, I felt immortal. I would *never* grow old.

At the age of three, I asked my mom if I could please have her sewing basket when she died. She was twenty-four. In my mind, my mom was old. Surely my request must have added a few gray hairs to her head.

Moving along several years, I felt sorry for my dad on his fortieth birthday. Poor guy, an old man with not much left for him. During that same time frame, I watched new mothers wheeling their babies in strollers downtown after school. Pitiful things, their lives were over. I asked myself, "Is there life after high school?"

At nineteen, I married an older man of twenty-seven. It all felt glamorous. Children came, and we were busy raising a family. I only had time to think about age once, when I passed into my forties. I already had a granddaughter. But ever youthful in my looks and energy, people often mistook me for her mother!

I would often overhear friends speak of men who had died at sixty-one or sixty-two and how they thought it was such a shame when men died so young. Sixty-*anything* seemed old to me at the time.

But not so when my brother died at sixty-four because he was young. Yes, *very* young. I was seventy-three.

Now I'm seventy-nine. I'm confined to my home most of the time with a degenerative disease, yet I don't feel old. I'm rounding the bend to eighty as are many of my friends. We haven't lost it yet. We all have various interests, great parties, lots of laughing and joking, board meetings with responsibilities . . .

So what is old? I don't know, I guess ninety-five. When I reach ninety-five, I suppose "old" will be more than one hundred. When I reach one hundred I will be too young and having too much fun to ever want to quit!

Phyllis Costello *(posthumously) was multitalented and loved to teach metaphysical truths. She walked her talk, believing that life always presents the best to you if you expect it to. Phyllis enjoyed her life right up to the end. She stayed actively involved in her local writers' guild, had a "firecracker personality," and mostly loved to make people laugh.*

Thirties Nostalgia Leaves Much to be Desired

by Gloria Burke

I don't like how fast these senior years are adding up, but I'd like to think of my next birthday as thirty-eight instead of eighty-three. Of course, it would be a lot easier to imagine if I'd just stop looking in the mirror!

Once I tried hanging a snapshot of me at age twelve on my bathroom mirror, thinking I might feel rejuvenated if I looked at myself as I was seventy years ago. It didn't help; there just wasn't any resemblance between that pretty blond twelve-year-old and the gray-haired woman who stared back at me.

When I was a kid, I could literally skip home from school, my long blond curls bouncing with every step. Those long curls were tempting to the boys. One of them was Carl Lemle, a fourth grade classmate who thought it was great fun to pull my curls. I trounced him squarely one day as a direct result of the boxing lessons that my cousin, Chuck Sturm, was giving me. Cousin Chuck was an amateur boxer and my grandmother had commandeered him to instruct me as to how to defend myself. He installed a punching bag from the rafters in our basement so he could teach me the ropes. One day when Carl pulled my curls as we were walking home from school, I punched him soundly in the stomach. He fell to the ground, crying, as I hurried on my way. He never tried to pull my hair again.

Nostalgia's not my thing, though. No way, no how would I ever want to go back to the way so many things were when I was growing up.

The part that's least nostalgic to me is the part about taking a bath only on Saturday nights. My mother was always first in the tub. Once she bathed, the rest of the family took turns—in the same water! A kettle full of hot water was kept heating on the stove to be added after each bath. I guess in today's world, we'd name it "recycling" or "conservation" day.

I don't feel at all nostalgic about having to wear day-old underwear either. In those days, we weren't given the option of changing every day. My grandmother was the family expert at giving our day-old clothes the "sniff test" to decide whether or not our garments could last one more wearing.

In my early teens, I was introduced to the girdle, a tortuous garment designed to inhibit natural bulges. Just to don it required herculean strength, as it had to be pulled, yanked, stretched, and tugged before it sat correctly on my already-overweight hips. Then once into it, its long garters were attached to thigh-high silk hose with seams that, in spite of my very best efforts, were never straight and always managed to fall down and crumple around my ankles.

Nostalgia about the good old days is definitely not my thing, especially when I recall some of the many inconveniences I was forced to "enjoy."

Gloria Burke ~ *It wasn't until Gloria Burke began teaching a class called "Writing Your Memories" in 1992 that her own writing career took off. She has taught English classes at the middle school, high school, and college levels for many years. At eighty-three, she still works. (419) 885-1413*

The Tell-Tale Truth about Trash

by Shmuel Shimshoni

What I don't know about trash would more than fill a dumpster, so I'll just stick to what I *do* know about the subject. Trash should never be taken lightly.

But when it becomes too heavy, you may suffer humiliation from having the garbage bag split its sides with silent laughter. Refuse can be handled in a number of ways, such as "Please take down the trash, honey," or "When do you plan on getting rid of the rubbish?" Or even, "When you go, take the garbage with you!"

Trash can be carried out, taken down, thrown away, chucked, carted off to a remote destination, incinerated, or packed up nicely in a TV carton and left on the curb till someone steals it. Or it could be dumped on an empty lot, buried in the ground, even tossed overboard from your yacht. It's a proven fact that trash produced in the average home will usually be heavier and of greater volume than the raw material you brought home from the supermarket.

Do you realize that the contents of your refuse bin reflects the character of your home? For instance, should a passerby rummage through your trash, they might very well get a fair idea of your spending habits. Are you thrifty? (Think about it.) Would they find inexpensive, but healthy, raw fruits and vegetables or the more costly brands of canned or frozen foods? Do you watch your diet, e.g., use date-spread instead of jam?

Do you toss out peelings rather than save them to produce valuable humus for your garden? Do you dispose of things that are still usable? Are your utility bills paid on time or does your trash contain third and fourth notices from suppliers?

Are you ecologically conscious? Wasteful? Or just plain lazy? Do you return bottles or trash them? (Don't forget, you already paid a deposit on them.) Also, if you throw out old backup computer discs, are you aware that they may still contain your passwords and bank account numbers, which could lead to identity theft?

When you place waste material in your garbage can, you may be abandoning it, but you're not entirely relinquishing ownership of it. How can I be so sure? I'm willing to bet that when you glance out of your window and notice somebody rummaging through your trash can you'll most certainly open the window and yell, "Hey, you! What do you think you're doing? Get away from *my* garbage!"

Why? Because you're still very much attached to your trash and all the sacred secrets it can tell about you and the manner in which you live.

Shmuel Shimshoni *is an eighty-year-old former electrician, master locksmith, pneumatic automation technician, and undertaker who enjoys fictionalizing and spicing up humorous stories. He lives in Israel, is a community volunteer, and insists he has plenty of "raw materials" to write about.*

Chapter 8:
SACRED MOMENTS

Three Strings

by Jack Riemer (As told by Gloria Loring)

*As told by keynote speaker **Gloria Loring** at the 2002 Starburst Inspirations' charity fund-raising luncheon*

On November 18, 1995, Itzhak Perlman gave a concert at Avery Fisher Hall at Lincoln Center in New York City, and those of us who have seen him either in person or on television know that he was stricken with polio as a very young child, and wears braces on his legs and walks with crutches.

When he comes onto a concert stage, he walks very slowly to his chair using his crutches. Then he puts the crutches down, arranges one foot back and one foot forward, leans down slowly, gets his violin, nods to the conductor, and starts to play. Audiences know this ritual and sit patiently with great respect, letting him have that quiet time to get himself settled.

On this particular night, something went wrong. After he played a few bars of a symphonic piece, one of his violin strings broke. You could hear it snap. It went off like gunfire across the hall. Everyone could hear it; the audience thought he would get up, go offstage and get another violin, or get this one restrung. But that's not what happened.

Itzhak Perlman stopped. The conductor stopped. He sat there for a few moments with his eyes closed, then nodded to the conductor to begin again, and he played the piece on three strings.

Anyone who knows anything about the violin knows you cannot play a symphonic piece on three strings. But Itzhak Perlman refused to know that. He played because he was in the moment, guided by the flow of his love for what he was doing. He played with such power and passion and purity that when he finished, people leapt to their feet, cheering and screaming to let him know that they had just heard something extraordinary.

With a sweet humility, he gestured for them to be quiet, wiped his brow, and said "You know, sometimes it's the artist's task to find out how much music you can make with what you have left."

Maybe that's the task for our lives also. Here's a man who trained all his life to play with four strings and suddenly he only had three. Yet that night he made music so memorable, so beautiful, so sacred it seemed to transcend anything he had ever done.

So maybe it's not just a task for artists. Maybe it's a task for all of us. To approach life giving it all we've got, and when things go wrong, to see how much music we can make with what have left.

[Reproduced with permission of Houston Chronicle Publishing Company via Copyright Clearance Center.]

Gloria Loring is a singer, songwriter, actress, and the author of four books for people with diabetes. An audience favorite as Liz Chandler from daytime TV's Days of Our Lives, *she is also an inspirational speaker for corporations and nonprofits. She is the recording artist of the #1 hit song* Friends and Lovers, *co-composer of television theme songs for* Diff'rent Strokes *and* Facts of Life, *and one of the few artists to sing two nominated songs at the Academy Awards.*

Picnics at Shady Nook

by David R. Weir

Among the earliest and most favorite memories with Gram were the summer picnics she and I shared alone together beside a tiny stream on the outskirts of our small Midwestern town.

I recall the shade of the towering elms overhanging the clear water near a bridge and hidden spot we called Shady Nook. Gram prepared for her special times with me by bringing a picnic basket packed full of my favorite peanut butter and jelly sandwiches, plus tasty goodies from her kitchen pantry. Afterwards, I'd toss the remaining crumbs from our feast into the slowly moving waters to lure excited guppies and minnows into a feeding frenzy. Observing my delight and giggles brought indescribable joy to Gram's face and we laughed for no other reason than laughter's joy. In quiet moments, I'd bask in the warmth of her adoration, knowing I was loved today and forever by my caring, doting grandmother.

Over the next few years the landscape of our community changed, and with these changes the idyllic setting of Shady Nook disappeared under what grown-ups called progress. Nonetheless, as a teenager I found myself returning to Shady Nook—or as near to it as I could get—to remember those loving times, and once even to cry my eyes out over the death of our family dog, who was hit by a passing car. Shady Nook was, after all, a place where one could feel love and not be embarrassed, wasn't it?

In the journey of life, there comes a time when we become aware of our own mortality, and with it, the people whose love helped guide us and make us who we are. As I look back at my childhood, growing up in a small Nebraska town during War World II, of course I see my maternal grandmother as that guiding, shaping love. Along with my mother's, it was the force that led me with its light through my formative preschool years while my father was away serving in the U.S. Navy. Later, when my father returned from the war and my parents gave me siblings, I learned the meaning of "sibling rivalry." But for the first four years of my life, I was the happy sole center of attention from two loving, doting women.

Gram was a resilient survivor of the Depression years. Her husband, Frank, had died of heart failure in 1932 after only fourteen years of marriage and just one child—my mother. Gram inherited Grandpa Frank's farm, which had been homesteaded by the family in the mid-1800s, and now grew mostly corn and soybeans. This was the sole source of income for Gram during those difficult years, and later. On grounds that remain unclear to this day, Gram was told she did not qualify for the Social Security benefits that later came along as part of Franklin Roosevelt's New Deal. As an adult, I later learned that Gram had received several proposals of marriage early in her widowhood, but that she'd chosen to remain single for the rest of her life—again, for reasons that would remain a mystery. But I think I now understand. Gram had one daughter who needed her love and help, and a grandson whose father was away at war and who also needed her love and help. What was life, if not a chance to help family first and foremost through the love that only family can know?

In my memory—which I know is accurate because love never lies—Gram never tired of doing things for or with me. She sewed my name in all my mittens and coats, allowed me to play in her attic with her antique doll set, and read the Twenty-third Psalm and other Bible stories to me while rocking on the swing hanging from the ceiling of her big porch. She made sure I was taken to the weekly story hour at our local Carnegie Library, and treated me to hot roast beef sandwiches at her favorite restaurant, Al's Café.

Gram would also let me water her flowers alongside the driveway, pick low-hanging apples from her backyard tree, and always assured me there was a safe place for me to take naps in her second bedroom when I got tired. She also let me listen to her big Emerson radio, propelled by the latest vacuum tube technology of the day.

My grandmother was also a big help to my mother, assisting with many household chores such as cooking, washing, sewing, ironing, and shopping. She also kept the latest news about the war at her fingertips, even while she served as the main calming influence upon my mother, who worried daily about my father's fate on a battle ship in the Pacific theater.

How Gram ever found time for herself, I don't know, but if she didn't, I know why. Time with those you love—even if they see it as your helping or serving them—is the best time there is in life. Nevertheless, Gram, who was known to her adult friends as Lillian, somehow maintained an active, productive social life in her church, neighborhood, and community at large through such volunteer agencies as the American Red Cross and the USO. She was as popular with the outside world as she was with us. Why am I not surprised?

Now fast-forward several generations. Today, it's *me* who's the doting grandparent of a young boy with big dreams and boundless energy. Will his exposure to the worldly world over time compromise his sweet innocence? Did it compromise mine? Must we always lose it?

To some degree, growing up always causes us to lose the sweet innocence that grown-ups see in children. And yet, what we manage to keep of it is the part that was protected and nourished by those who loved us when we were young. So now I'm determined to find— for my grandson and for myself—a "Shady-Nook" that he and I can share together. It is only there that I will be able to keep my grandmother's memory alive in the sacred moments that only love can make.

David R. Weir *is a sixty-eight-year-old father and grandfather who is an avid reader, golfer, table tennis player, swimmer, volunteer pianist, hiker, and traveler since his retirement from a long career in public health administration and related consulting work. David grew up in a small town in Nebraska and now spends most of his time with loved ones in California.*

May Day Friends Forever

by Patricia Westerfield

April showers bring May flowers and May first commemorates a cherished tradition that I love to recall from childhood.

Every May Day, I'd make small flower baskets out of colored construction paper, and later my mom would pick flowers for me to place inside them. Then I'd quietly sneak up to each of our neighbors' houses, leave a basket of flowers on their front doorsteps, ring their doorbells, and quickly run and hide. Eager to see and hear their surprised reactions, I'd peek out from behind the bushes without making a sound. The neighbors would always smile when they discovered the May basket, look around, and usually say, "Thank you!" I never knew if they could actually see me hiding, but I sure liked to believe that they couldn't.

I was twenty-one when I got married, and the first home my husband and I lived in was a small duplex with a carport and tiny patch of grass. One day in early winter, he surprised me by digging up a small area on the side of the carport where he strung wire and planted a bed of sweet peas. By May of that year, we enjoyed a glorious wall of lovely blooms! They were so fragrant, colorful, and beautiful that we took bouquets to everyone we knew.

Soon afterwards, our first baby boy was born and we moved into a house. We lived there for ten years and always enjoyed a profusion of sweet-scented sweet peas each spring. As soon as our children could walk, every year on the first day of May they began the tradition of surprising neighbors by leaving a basket of sweet peas on their doorsteps. We continued this custom after moving to an even larger house and rounding out our family to five children. For over twenty years, the children—even as teenagers—carried out this special tradition.

Eventually, I joined the Junior Women of the Contemporary Club, a local social-service club in which many young women participated and where lasting friendships were formed. One year, four of us happened to be pregnant at the same time, including Jan Fowler (author-editor of this book), who was also a member of Juniors. In fact, she and I delivered our babies within one day of each other. Our baby boys—my son Michael and her son Randy—were not only in the same hospital nursery together, but also grew up attending the same schools and joining the same Cub Scout pack, which I led as den mother.

One week when Jan arrived to pick up Randy at my home following a Cub Scout meeting, she admired all the beautiful sweet peas that covered our swimming pool fence. She was noticeably enchanted by them because of their delicate beauty and fragrance.

May first was not far away, and that's when Jan received her first bunch of sweet peas. Michael delivered them in a coffee can with water, not a basket, and of course rang the doorbell before he ran and hid behind her tall hedge. When Jan answered the door, she was surprised and delighted. She had a good hunch she knew who they were from.

It has now been more than forty years since Michael's first delivery of flowers, and Jan and I have *never forgotten to surprise each other* every May Day since!

Each year, she quietly sneaks up to my front porch where she leaves a coffee can overflowing with her beautiful roses, and I, in turn, tiptoe up to *her* front porch to deliver a coffee can of colorful, sweet-smelling sweet peas.

She and I never see each other at any time throughout the year, nor do we ever even call or send one another cards. Yet we remain May Day friends forever . . . the fragrance of our enduring friendship lingers long after the flowers are gone.

Patricia Westerfield is a retired kindergarten teacher. She has been married to David, her college sweetheart and "the grower of sweet peas," for fifty-three years. She is the mother of five, mother-in-law to five, and grandmother of fifteen. She and Jan Fowler have known each other for more than four decades.

Washing Dishes in the Great Northwoods

by Anne E. Haugan

Have you ever considered washing dishes to be a joy? Well, in northern Minnesota at our picturesque campsite located on Norwegian Bay of Lake Vermilion, dishwashing can be an absolute delight! And after sixty-five years of experience, I do consider myself to be an expert on the subject. Even though, more often than not, I admit that doing dishes can be a task of drudgery, washing dishes at *our* rocky shore campsite is a totally different experience.

While sitting on my stool observing the scenic sights and sounds of nature surrounding me—with a dishpan of boiling water set on the rocks before me—this mundane job is transformed into a joyful, exciting experience.

First, I'm captivated as I watch the beautiful male hummingbird whirl onto the feeder, then return to the birch branch. There he waits for a female or young hummer to come feed, then attacks. He considers himself King of the Nectar. Then other songbirds flit from branch to branch, searching for their meal of juicy insects. Their sweet-toned songs resemble a melodious choir.

Osprey chicks suddenly call from the high nest atop the dead white pine on the island opposite our campsite. "We're hungry for a fresh fish meal!" they seem to plead. Then when I see Mama or Papa Osprey land on the nest, the desperate calls of the chicks cease. Watching the eagles soar overhead using their spectacular flying skills poses a guessing game. Where will their eagle-sharp vision lead them to find their next meal?

Mother Mallard and Mother Merganser glide quietly along the shore with their broods of ducklings following close behind like shadows. Mother ducks warily watch for dangers while they teach their young how to catch food. There is Mother Snapping Turtle, large and silent, with only her head visible above the water. And ever so stealthily, a mink sneaks along the rocky shores. At the same hour every evening, Papa Beaver cruises by. I wonder where he'll go tonight to chomp down a tree with his large beaver incisors.

While the call of loons is taken for granted on northern lakes, the challenge is to listen carefully to discern whether the call is a hoot, a wail, a tremolo, or a yodel. Can we guess by their behavior what might be going on in their lives? Suddenly, the attentive chipmunk becomes my companion, ready to assist with any crumbs left on the dirty dishes. The greatest joy is looking up to find him in a frozen position, staring me down.

I purposely choose to carry out this camp chore in the evenings. Only then can I watch the setting sun and reflect on how the sky is uniquely streaked with rainbow hues. The timing of the sunset is also intriguing as daylight lengthens. Then after midsummer, the days become shorter while the sun moves south and hides behind Fire Island.

I'll admit that Northwoods dishwashing is not always a joy. For if done too late in the evening hours, there might be a battle with mosquitoes. Or if it's raining, cold, or windy, this camp job could turn into a somewhat unpleasant chore. But there are so many joyful memories of sacred moments to flood my heart and mind that I quickly forget the occasional unpleasant inconveniences.

Whatever . . . I've gotta get these dishes done. You betcha!!!

Anne E. Haugan is a wife, mother, and retired teacher who is active in church, Befriender Ministry, and social concerns. She is an avid environmentalist who has done camp counseling in Boundary Waters Canoe Area Wilderness. Her family enjoys their own campsite in Minnesota Northwoods on Norwegian Bay of Lake Vermilion. ahaugan@usfamily.net

Please Keep Those Phones Ringing!

by Shirley A. Lamb

As the mother of eight children who lives a considerable distance away from most of them, you can imagine the special way in which my spirits are uplifted whenever I hear their familiar cheery voices over the phone. Be it Mother's Day or any day, whenever I hear "Hi, Mom!" I melt with joy over the special bond and connection my children and I share.

As a small child growing up in the '40s, I recall how my own mother was not so fortunate because she could only afford to call her mother twice a year—at Christmas and on Mother's Day. In those days, we communicated mostly through letters. Remember when stamps only cost three cents apiece?

This year for Mother's Day, my wonderful husband, Jim, took me out to dinner the night before—my choice—where he surprised me with a lovely musical card and to my delight, a bottle of my favorite perfume, Red Door. Our early celebration now left all day Sunday free for the telephone "visits" that I hoped would come.

Sure enough, first thing in the morning my fun began.

First, I received "Happy Mother's Day" calls from three of my sons, all of whom lived far from my home in northern California. Two phoned me from their homes in Miami, Florida, and the third, a truck driver who happened to be driving through Arkansas at the time, called from his cell. I had great fun getting caught up on their family news, which always does wonders for my heart. Though I'd already received cards and gifts of money from most of the kids, actually hearing their voices provided magical moments.

Since I had nothing special planned for the day, I happily busied myself with routine household chores, while remaining keyed up and filled with anticipation. Later, when I reentered the kitchen from the garage where I'd been out doing laundry, I noticed the message button on my phone flashing. The excitement mounted. Now who could it be next?

This time, the call was from my youngest daughter, Sue, also a mother, so I eagerly called her back with a Mother's Day wish of my own. During the next twenty minutes or so, we both laughed as she brightened my day with news that her two teenage daughters had given both her and her sister foot massages as their Mother's Day gifts. Already roused with chuckles, I smiled long after I hung up and had returned to my laundry.

Talking with Sue reminded me that it was she who'd first introduced me to the long distance phone card that only charges 2.9 cents a minute. I recalled how it was a nuisance to use at first, but easy once I mastered the process. Before dialing a number, I'm required to punch in twenty-two *other* numbers beforehand. By now, of course I've memorized the codes so it only takes a few seconds to place a long-distance call. And 2.9 cents makes me feel so thrifty I don't even think twice about calling one of my children or a friend and chatting away for half an hour—it's only ninety cents. Gradually, I learned to purchase thirty dollars' worth of calls at a time, which buys 1020 minutes and lasts me four months. Not too bad money-wise!

Back in the 1940s, in the days when my mother called her own mother, a three-minute long-distance phone call cost three dollars. Once you'd talked for three minutes, an operator interrupted to say, "Your three minutes are now up" so you knew the call would be more expensive if you stayed on the line any longer.

At that time, my parents' mortgage payment was fifty-four dollars a month, including taxes, which meant that three dollars was approximately 5 percent of their mortgage payment. Based on a a thousand dollars rent or mortgage payment in today's market, 5 percent would be fifty dollars. I highly doubt we'd make as many calls if they cost fifty dollars each.

Back in 1953 when I was first married, I couldn't call my mother when our first child was born because we didn't even have a phone. It simply didn't fit into our budget. So my husband called her collect, at her request, from a pay phone. Actually, we couldn't afford a phone until after our second child was born. I recall that the day when I went into labor, I had to quickly run next door to use my neighbor's phone to notify my husband to please hurry home from work.

Later, when he became a salesman out on the road and I was left at home with two small children, we finally installed a phone just in case of emergency. In those days, one phone was all anyone had in the average household. Our rent was sixty-five dollars per month and the phone service ran two dollars and fifty cents.

When I mentioned this story to my present husband, Jim (we met and married after we were both widowed), he recalled that in 1951 while stationed in Korea, he called his mother collect and the call cost her fifty-five dollars for three minutes, roughly the equivalent of a monthly mortgage!

Today we have three phones in the house, plus our cell phone. I enjoy knowing I can afford to talk with family and friends whenever I please without being financially concerned. Affordable phone service is such a blessing these days. So please keep those phones ringing!

Shirley A. Lamb is a seventy-six-year-old retired medical transcriptionist, mother of nine and grandmother of nine. She lives with husband, Jim, on "Lamb's Roost" in the foothills of Yosemite National Park, where they have a small boysenberry farm. She enjoys writing, being active in community theater, painting rocks, and serving as president of her church women's guild. (559) 658-8587

The First Time I Met Stella

by Else Jacobs

My son and his wife did not want to know whether their first baby would be a boy or girl, but a few months before the birth, I had a vision that the baby would be a girl. My vision was a short one, but was so strong and convincing that I had no doubt. And later, when I shared my experience with my son, he stoically replied, "Yes, you are 50 percent right!"

And so Stella, a beautiful, healthy baby girl, was born in January 2005. Two months later, I paid a visit to see her. For me, meeting my granddaughter for the first time was an historical event. I found it touching to watch my son lovingly change her diaper, carefully swaddle her, then hand her over to her mother for some breastfeeding. I was next in line for some special grandmotherly holding and cuddling.

As I lovingly put Stella's face up to mine, felt her warmth, and held her close, I noticed that she had the sweetest baby smell. I looked straight into her face and our eyes met for just a few moments. Although brief, it was as if her telling eyes were saying "I know who you are."

Then an annoying hiccough came up in her, making her little head and body twitch. This occurred quite frequently, and when it did, her otherwise relaxed face appeared distraught and worried.

Having studied traditional Chinese medicine both in America and at the Xi Yuan Hospital in Beijing under Dr. Lu years earlier, I suddenly remembered what he taught us about hiccoughs. He said, "Place your index finger on the tip of the nose of the person who has the hiccough for just a few seconds, exert light pressure, and the hiccough will go away."

But Stella's head was rapidly moving in different directions, much faster than my finger could keep up with. Each time I would reach her nose, her head would jerk away again. Finally, after several attempts I succeeded, and—*Voila!*—those hiccoughs went away as quickly as they came!

Stella seemed relieved and gave me a big smile, as if to say, "Thank you, Grandma!" A great peace then settled over her and she fell fast asleep in my arms. Later, I handed her back to her mother to lay her in her crib.

Stella is now four years old. Next time I see her, I will tell her about our first meeting. I will also remind her often about what wonderful fun it is to be a grandmother!

__Else Jacobs__ is a native of Norway, where she taught elementary school before moving to California to work as a fitness instructor at the Golden Door Spa in Escondido. She has studied yoga, tai chi, and chi gong in India and China, is a certified reflexologist and massage therapist, and has had stories published in The Road Taken.

Saved by a Hat

by Geraldine Salvatorelli

The few times I ever heard my dad swear was when he was directing his words at the television screen, such as when the president said something he didn't agree with. Until this one calm evening, the evening when my fourteen-year-old brother and his best friend, Mickey Silane, playfully pushed their homemade boulder-sized snowball over and off the roof of our apartment building.

As the boys looked down, they were horrified to see their giant snowball graze the brim of Dad's hat just as he was turning the corner of Briggs and East 201st Street on his way home from work.

"What the hell?" Dad shouted as he flew up the four flights of stairs to our four-room walk-up, which he usually proudly referred to as his "honeymoon apartment." But this time, there was a different kind of stars in his eyes as he encountered the two boys anxiously racing down several flights from the roof with the look of nervous terror in their eyes. Their massive snowball had missed Dad by a hair. "Damn, what the hell happened? he growled. "I could have been *killed*!"

Immediately, we all gathered in the family kitchen with Mom. Until that night, it was clear that the most egregious act the boys had ever committed was to steal a roast beef from the oven and eat it before dinner.

Everyone remained silent. Dad was the only one who spoke. "They almost *killed* me. You could have *killed* me!" he ranted. Dad uttered the word *kill* over and over like the needle on a warped record. The boys were so scared and horrified by the possible consequences of their playful actions—a coma, concussion, or death itself—that each time the word *kill* was mentioned, they shuddered and apologized all over again.

And though Dad did say, "If I ever catch either one of you up there again . . ." he never lodged any further blame or punishment against them. In fact, it was quite the opposite, and soon, feelings of relief and glee took over; we also noticed that my father never removed his hat that night.

Many years passed until one day when Dad was out shoveling snow and nearly fainted. The doctor who treated him was none other than my brother's childhood friend, Mickey Silane, now known as Michael Silane, M.D., vascular surgeon. He diagnosed Dad as needing a heart valve replacement and promptly referred him to the operating physician, who in turn asked Dad to choose between a pig valve or a mechanical valve.

Dad, who is now ninety-three, selected a mechanical valve, and became the medical profession's "poster child" for successfully tolerating Coumadin, the blood thinner medication required to prevent blood clots from forming in those with prosthetic heart valves.

And my brother's best childhood friend, Mickey Silane, got to do what he was always meant to do—prolong and *save* life.

Geraldine Salvatorelli *is a memoir writer and former television assistant and researcher, stand-up comedian, and piano performer. To read her many stories—including* "Green is the Color of My True Love's Eyes," "Three Shots Fired!" *plus one about Grandma Antoinetta, who wore shoes and stockings every day, even to the beach—visit www.geraldeena.com or Geraldeena@aol.com*

Slivovitz

by Ruth Rosenthal

I will never forget the strong and fiery taste of my father's favorite drink. It was nearly two hundred proof, made from distilled plums, and called "slivovitz." To him, it was just an ordinary part of breakfast, to be enjoyed along with his coffee—stronger than a witch's brew, of course—dark rye bread, and salty herring. But to me, it was a searing jolt of energy that coursed through mouth and gullet till it blazed a heated trail through my entire body, fast as mysterious echoes from beyond.

It was only after my mother died that Pop and I found ourselves alone in his kitchen. His whole life, he had lived only to work, but now was both widowed *and* retired. I was his only daughter and yet he had never before had a personal conversation or even shared moments of his life with me.

So here we were alone and together, me now an adult, and he in the year before he followed Mom to the grave. What would our connection have been that day were it not for the magic of slivovitz?

"You like?" he asked eagerly.

"YES!" I answered enthusiastically.

"You want more?" He waited with anticipation.

To think that I might have stayed upstairs, indulging myself in the comfort of the king-sized bed, and never be downstairs in the kitchen, allowing him this question. I could have simply nurtured the hangnail that had been pestering me ever since I left home. For that matter, I could have avoided this entire blizzard of my mind and body and flown back to California the day before.

In those days, we didn't know enough to speak openly about death and dying. My mother had only spoken of Marilyn Monroe's dying and how sad it was that she was so young. And all this while, my mother's cancer was pulsing within her, causing her to softly say, "It jumps like a baby," as she gently touched her stomach.

And so I didn't hesitate a second to tell my father what I knew he needed to hear.

"YES!" I loudly enthused to his offer for a second drink.

It went down in one heated gulp, no less intense than the first one. The only difference was that this time, I was better prepared for what to expect.

Then came his offer of a third drink. My father had warmed up to me for the first time ever! Of course, I could have stopped, but I knew better.

That was our very last time together . . . Thank goodness for slivovitz.

Ruth Rosenthal *established a poetry group for psychiatric patients at Marin General Hospital, California, where amazing changes were noted as patients—some of whom had never written before—expressed their deepest feelings and discovered their hidden joys. Ruth has authored* Like Fallen Snow, *and* Maybe Shirts are Easier: A Path Back to Life. *(559) 240-5533*

A Drawer Full of Memories

by Anne J. Basile

As the song goes, "The weather outside is frightful, but the fire is so delightful . . ." Yes, this is definitely the kind of day to stay indoors, so I might as well do something useful, like straighten up those dresser drawers. It's a job I've been putting off. I can't even remember what's in them anymore; it's been so long.

Now, suddenly, I'm spreading a beautifully quilted apron on the bed and remembering that trip to the Florida Everglades many years ago. I recall admiring it in a shop window, then learning that the store was out of stock. With my curiosity aroused, I asked where it had come from and learned that Seminole Indian women had made them in their village. The beautiful apron had beckoned me from the showcase window and I knew I simply had to have one.

I somehow managed to pry directions from the store clerk, who advised me not to go. But determined, I found the village, parked the car, and crossed over a footbridge alone. The area was strangely empty, except for a little boy standing in a field. He gazed at me briefly, then turned and ran away. I quickly followed him and came to a clearing where a group of women sat chatting at their sewing machines beneath a palm-thatched chickee, a small house built on stilts.

When I called to them, I was met with sudden silence and stony stares. It was then that I realized why the store clerk had cautioned me. This was not a shop. It was their home and I had intruded. This apron in my hand was actually purchased in another store, but it reminds me of the proud history of the Seminole culture, which deserves understanding and respect.

A second apron folded in the same drawer was a souvenir from the Folk Art Center near Asheville, North Carolina. With its colorful quilted bib and pocket sewn onto a flowered skirt, I was reminded of the mountain people, whose special talents are passed from generation to generation to ensure their preservation. And there at the bottom of the drawer was a one-piece favorite bathing suit, reminding me that both styles *and* my figure have sure changed over the years.

The next drawer contained a box of faintly scented faded handkerchiefs, which transported me all the way back to high school. I had had a secret crush on the captain of the basketball team, so I asked the whole team to autograph my handkerchief. As I traced their embroidered signatures with my finger, I wondered where they all were today.

Now, what's this? A stack of colored dressy gloves to be worn with matching hats and purses. Who in the world wears these anymore? One white leather pair was a beautiful and special gift from my husband, bought on his tour of duty overseas following the war.

Another drawer was stashed with dozens of T-shirts representing our many travels. One was imprinted with North Carolina lighthouses, another with Mexican hats, still another with a colorful Indian headdress, several with college logos, and even one with the Mud Hens of Toledo. And now here's my baby book with a lock of my blond hair tucked inside! Oh, my goodness, what's this wrapped in brown paper and snugly tucked in the corner? It's *The Marriage Manuel,* written in 1935 by Hannah and Abraham Stone. Oh yes, I now remember, a thoughtful gift from my mother-in-law. It must have been filled with wondrous advice and wisdom; we've been married fifty-five years!

And so what began as a dreaded chore today soon became a most pleasant stroll down "Memory Lane." The unexpected discovery of so many forgotten treasures has filled my heart with a warm and gentle glow. I look forward to opening those last three drawers, but I'm afraid they will have to wait until tomorrow.

I'm still savoring the joyful surprise discoveries of today.

Anne J. Basile, *now in her mid-eighties, was a librarian at Davis College in Toledo, Ohio. She began writing her memoirs several years ago for her children, grandchildren, and great grandchildren. Anne is both founder and president of her local chapter of the Church and Synagogue Library Association. (419) 882-1610*

Sweetie Pie

by Lois J. Miller

My husband, Harold, had been suffering from blood circulation problems and the day finally came when it became medically necessary for him to have both legs amputated. After such a life-changing event, one would have expected everything afterwards to be a "downer," right? Well, I'm very happy to say that such was far from the case with us.

Fortunately, we'd been blessed with a wonderful marriage and when Harold became disabled, we seemed to grow even closer. In fact, we enjoyed far more happy moments than sad and were still able to live a life that was very close to normal.

For example, we continued to enjoy our vacation mobile home and bass boat at Temple Bar on the Arizona side of Lake Mead. Harold was still able to drive the boat because he'd had it specially equipped and customized with manual hand controls.

Every so often he and I would take a day to run errands, buy dry goods, and shop for groceries. Sometimes we'd head for Henderson, Nevada, by way of Hoover Dam, but on this particular day, we drove to Kingman, Arizona, about eighty miles away. There, we stopped at a Walmart where I pulled into a handicapped parking spot, removed Harold's wheelchair from the back of our vehicle, and started to set it up next to his passenger door.

While I was occupied with this task, a woman had returned to her pickup truck that happened to be parked right next to us. Just as I was bending over the wheelchair to make sure it was fully opened and stabilized, Harold asked me to "just stay put" for a minute because he noticed something in my hair. Then he leaned out from his perch in our SUV and ran his hand over and through my hair as if searching for the culprit on my head. And the next thing I knew, he quite playfully and unexpectedly smooched me right on the top of my head!

As we both straightened up, the lady next to us unexpectedly turned to me and said, "You really have a sweetie pie there." Of course, I agreed and replied that I knew I did. And with that, she turned around rather quickly, almost as if embarrassed that she had ever spoken or been privy to a tender moment that should have remained private. Then before we knew it, without any further word, the lady climbed into her pickup and was gone.

As I write this, it occurs to me that that lady in the parking lot will probably never know that without her casual remark about my "Sweetie Pie," I might never have given Harold's smooch on my head quite as much importance. But because she took the time to make a comment, the memory of this particular incident has lingered in my mind over the years as a very special moment.

And she was right! I did indeed have a very special "Sweetie Pie."

Lois J. Miller is a seventy-seven-year-old widow who retired after forty-five years in the business world. She took a writing course for children's stories before she retired, and since then has published ten stories (all included in four books) in the Lulu.com system. P.O. Box #35, Maynard, Iowa 50655

The Pacifier

by Dora Klinova

My nine-month-old baby grandson, Dennis, had a heavy cold and hadn't been able to sleep well for several nights. But finally, he seemed to be feeling better and played peacefully on the carpet. His mother, my daughter, lay down on the sofa near him and wearily closed her eyes, trying to relax.

Soon Dennis became bored with his toys and looked up at Mama. But she slept. He needed Mama at this moment! Unable to walk yet, he crawled to the sofa, pulled himself up onto his feet by grabbing the furniture, and approached Mama's face. He pulled her nose, hands, and hair. But Mama did not react. She still did not open her eyes.

The baby had reached the limit of his resources. He shook Mama and tugged at her, but still no reaction. Then the little one finally decided to use his most powerful tool, the pacifier that he held in his mouth. Mama could never resist this most pleasurable thing in the world.

Dennis resolutely pulled the pacifier from his own mouth, then squeezed and pushed it between Mama's lips. At the time, Dennis' teeth and gums were tender and had been bothering him, so when he kept the pacifier in his mouth, it was not the soft nipple he sucked on, but the opposite hard side. This was what helped him to scratch his gums and soothe his cutting teeth.

So now, of course, he plunged the pacifier into Mama's mouth with the same hard side. Mama couldn't resist this generous gesture. Laughingly, she soon grabbed her baby to her, hugging and kissing him.

You can ask me, "So what? It's just a routine cute baby's trick that happens so often. Why write about it?"

No, this is not a story about a cute baby's prank. It is much deeper. You will admit that in life, it's not always so easy to attract somebody else's attention. We really must often be inventive to make people think about us when they don't want to, and to not allow them to move us aside as an unwanted object.

This baby solved a complicated problem: to gain Mama's attention against her will. Dennis neither cried nor yelled. He used everything available to him to reach his goal and did it artistically and graciously. For him, it was somehow strategic diplomacy. Instead of pestering, he made his tired mother laugh. It lifted her mood so much that she called me in San Diego to tell this story.

Bravo, my baby! I would give you an A+ for this experiment.

Dora Klinova is an award-winning writer and poet whose works have been published in newspapers and magazines, and performed on stage. Her book, A Melody from an Immigrant's Soul, *is the heartfelt story of a Russian Jewish immigrant.* dorishka2000@yahoo.com *or (619) 667-0925*

Memories are Made of This

by Nancy C. Lydick

It was a fantastic October weekend in Indiana—simply ideal! Clear blue autumn skies, a gentle cool breeze, warm glowing sunshine, plus the crisp smell of recently harvested crops in the air. Football weather—my favorite time of the year in Indiana.

On this great day, a Saturday, I felt inspired to visit several of my relatives. My husband, Edward, and I smiled and nodded, knowing that no time could ever feel more perfect than now. So first, we set out for Aunt Fran and Uncle John's home in Noblesville, where we knew we could count on Fran serving delicious ham with tasty green beans and potatoes. Had this been a little earlier in the season, she would have also served their juicy, homegrown Indiana tomatoes, which was my all-time favorite meal. Fran and John's warmth and hospitality to us turned out to be every bit as delightful as we had expected.

After lunch, we drove approximately three hours south to see Uncle Frank and Aunt Mickey at their home on the bank of White River. I still have fond memories of the days when my granny's house used to be right next door. A particular highlight of that visit was the joviality of sitting at their kitchen table drinking coffee while Uncle Frank and Edward gleefully exchanged fishing stories. Afterwards, we followed Frank outside to watch as he fed the wild ducks and geese living on the island. What an exhilarating sight to see them walking the path straight to his back door!

When the time came for us to leave, we returned to Aunt Fran and Uncle John's to spend the night. And of course our visit with them would never have been complete without their nightly bridge game. It was always the women versus the men. Aunt Fran really loved to playfully tease and rub it in when the women came out winners.

On Sunday morning, we bid them goodbye and drove north on the thirty-minute trip to Arcadia to visit Aunt Leota and Uncle Walter, my dad's brother, who lived on a farm where sheep were raised. This was a special spot which I always enjoyed visiting from the time I was a youngster. The food was worth the trip too, usually chicken and noodles. Leota and Walter always made us feel so welcome. After our lunch and catching up on all the family news, it was time to head home.

All in all, we had two great days, spent with some very nice people in a time and place I really loved. And the best thing is, I can take this trip over and over and never leave my chair. Just like today. All these good folks are long gone, but they will never be truly gone as long as I can visit them in my mind. They're all there, along with the feel of the cool breeze on my arms, the sun on my back, and the smell of the crisp October day.

Yes, memories are made of this and aren't we lucky to have them?

Nancy C. Lydick is a seventy-eight-year-old happily married housewife and mother of five sons who lives with her husband and two spoiled dogs. She divides her time between writing dog stories, life stories, playing pool, and attending senior dances with her husband. 1420 Pleasant Pointe Circle, Bryant, AR 72022

Chapter 9:
WHEN DREAMS COME TRUE

The Tunnel Tree

by Klaus Penning

When I was ten, my hobbies included collecting pictures from grown-ups' cigarette packs. It was an advertising gimmick to put pictures in those packs. They showed marvelous and unusual places like the Leaning Tower of Pisa, the Grand Canyon, the Eiffel Tower, and so on. There were about fifty pictures in all to be collected, and you could purchase an album at tobacco stores to put them in.

My dad smoked about one pack a day, and at that time back in Germany, a pack held only six cigarettes. I didn't smoke, of course, but I was a dreamer. I'd look at those pictures and see myself on top of the Eiffel Tower or sailing under the Golden Gate bridge.

The picture that fascinated me the most, however, was of a tree so big that it had a tunnel in it. You could drive right through it with an automobile. It seemed impossible, but there it was; the picture showed a car driving through the tree! The back of the picture explained that this giant of a tree was in a national park somewhere in the state of California in the United States of America.

I grew older. World War II raced over Europe, affecting my life just as it did everyone else's in Germany. I became a soldier for my country and spent four years in a Russian POW camp. When I returned to Germany after the war, I finished my education, married, and had a daughter. To support my family I worked as a bricklayer, a trade I'd learned in the Russian POW camp. It was hard work, but it paid well. Work of this kind was plentiful because Germany was trying to rebuild. I was an adult now, no longer free to dream, but I still thought about that picture of the fabulous tree.

Housing was a big problem in Germany then. We lived with three people crowded into one room. Then one morning on my way to work I saw a poster at a streetcar station announcing: *Refugees from East Germany! Build yourself a new life in the USA. For more information write to the U.S. Consulate in Dusseldorf.*

After thinking it over for several weeks, I told my wife I thought we should do it. So we applied for emigration to America, filled out the forms, and had a personal interview. Of the many questions we were asked, one threw us: "Where would you like to live in the U.S.?" Neither of us knew anything really about U.S. geography. But then I remembered the tunnel tree of my childhood. It was in California, wasn't it? I mentioned the tree to the emigration counselor, and he agreed that it had to be in California. He told us he could try to find us a place near Yosemite, the great national park. In fact, after checking his papers, he suggested a city called Fresno. There was a Lutheran Church there willing to sponsor us—more good fortune.

In March of 1957, we boarded the refugee ship that would take us to New York. From there we flew to Fresno. Our first year was difficult because we didn't know as much English as we should have. I worked on a turkey ranch, but later that year I was able to buy our first car, a 1953 Chevy. The first trip we took in it, of course, was to that magical tree in Yosemite. An adult now, I was able to fulfill my childhood dream: I drove my family *through* that tree, and all of us fell in love with the great national park that protected it. Later, with a new wife and a new career, I found myself working in Yosemite itself, and even now, I work as a part-time tour guide after retirement, joyfully sharing that tree with others.

I often marvel as I think of the little picture that so influenced my life.

Who said that a child's dreams cannot come true?

Klaus Penning *is eighty-three years old. He was born in Germany, served in the German Army during World War II, and was a POW in* *the Ukraine until 1949. In 1957, he emigrated to the U.S., where he worked as a farm laborer, operated his own sign business, and served on the Chamber of Commerce board. After retirement, he worked as a ski instructor and tour guide in Yosemite. Klaus27@gmail.com*

Aqua and Beautiful

by Carol Mann

I t was the summer of 1953—my sixteenth year—when freedom arrived! I had found the key to escaping the cloistered parental walls. The key—aqua and beautiful—brought a vicarious smile to my father's face, anguish to my mother's, and sheer joy to mine. It was worth every dollar.

I had always been taught to save. So through several years of serious effort, I did my best to stockpile money from birthdays, Christmases, and Confirmation. I collected bottles, cut the grass, and dusted. Baby-sitting, however, was the golden goose of money-making.

A lucky break occurred for me when a university professor, his wife, and family became our new neighbors and moved in across the street. They loved to entertain. So whenever they hosted a dinner party, I saw dollar signs (also headaches). My fate for an evening? To be sequestered downstairs in their recreation room with four little girls. Keeping their daughters entertained and preventing them from running upstairs to interrupt the party challenged my finer talents, but for this I received the bonus pay of fifty cents an hour.

Each Saturday, my father would then drive me to the Manufacturers and Traders Trust Company Bank in Buffalo, New York, with my hard-earned dollars. I watched attentively as the bank teller carefully entered each small deposit in my tiny passbook with black ink, then stamped the date. Once home again, I was always careful to safeguard my prized passbook in a special box reserved for teenage treasures.

My father was born in 1900 and grew up swept away in the wonder and excitement of the Automobile Age. Not having fathered any sons, he chose to nurture in his youngest daughter—*me*—a profound and absorbing interest in cars: Fords, Chevys, Oldsmobiles, Dodges, Hudsons, and Studebakers. I noticed cars everywhere and dreamt of having my own.

I recall how Dad always advised, "Be good to your car and it will be good to you." He also said, "If you want a car, you will have to earn it, for we can't afford to buy you one."

My mother came to view cars as necessary evils. And a vehicle in the hands of her youngest definitely made her nervous.

During my sophomore year, I successfully completed driver's training at Williamsville Central High School. Now fully armed with my Certificate of Completion, plus my bank book, I felt that the big event was approaching and could not be far off. I had accumulated $350, was trained, and ready.

Each evening, my father and I would intently read the automobile ads in the *Buffalo Evening News*. At last, an ad that made my heart race leapt from the page—a 1949 Studebaker coupe that was precisely the right price. The car was only four years old.

My teenage brain spun!

My mother sighed a long-suffering sigh. The inevitable, she knew, was coming.

Dad and I went to look at the car, and oh, what a sight! An aqua coupe. A sleek, pointed hood. A radio. Futuristic windows. Real chrome bumpers. I was in heaven . . .

The bank account may have emptied out, but this gorgeous little Studebaker became mine. Although they worried, they fretted, they lectured, my parents somehow managed to survive my first car. I believe they were secretly proud that I'd earned the money myself.

So was I!

Carol Mann, seventy-four, is a retired "educator-turned-writer" whose work has been published in both literary journals and magazines. She currently serves on the board of directors of the National League of American Pen Women, Palm Springs, California Branch. cstanfield@ dc.rr.com

Farm Girl Goes Hollywood

by JoAnn Fitzgibbons

Faith is the substance of things hoped for, the evidence of things not seen.

Hebrews 11:1

My dear and wonderful sister, Bobbie Ruth Jordan, always had faith. In fact, from the day she was born, it may have been *all* she had.

Bobbie was born with cerebral palsy and faced the daily challenges of learning to walk, talk, and carry out routine self-care. But as much as she tried her best and struggled to keep up with classmates in school, she was unable to continue beyond the tenth grade. However, Bobbie's personal resolve was *to never quit*. Deep down inside, she felt as normal as everyone else in our southern Georgia rural community.

During the long days at home while friends and family were occupied with school and farm duties that she could not assist with, Bobbie began to occupy her time by reading Hollywood celebrity magazines. Soon she began daydreaming that one day she would move to California, fall in love with and marry a movie star.

Although we cannot see faith, it is a very real force that works on our behalf.

Through a series of life events, Bobbie moved to Atlanta, Georgia, to work at a facility for handicapped individuals. Then, in order to be close to me, she moved out to southern California and began a life for herself here. So far, at least part of Bobbie's dream had come true.

William, on the other hand, was born in South Dakota, but he and his family moved to Hollywood when he was a young child.

There, he played in the back lots at the 20th Century Fox Studio where his dad worked as a security guard. William always enjoyed and appreciated being part of the excitement and adventure of the privileged movie community, and knew that one day he wanted to become an actor.

As he grew up, William studied hard and made the most of every opportunity to display his talents, skills, and abilities. And eventually, luck did indeed land him in a few episodes of the TV western, *Rawhide*. From then on, William's career bloomed! His six foot six frame and rugged good looks ushered him into movie roles, commercials, stage productions, and television. He chose Loren Ewing as his stage name, joined the Screen Actors' Guild, and had many film, television, and stage credits. He had arrived!

But one day, during the filming of a western scene, Loren had an unfortunate accident. He was kicked by a horse, incurred a serious head injury, then developed unfortunate complications that required him to move close to a rehabilitation center in Pomona, California. And that's when faith intervened because it happened to be the same rehabilitation center where Bobbie worked every day. Soon, they rode the same bus to and from the center, met each other, and quickly became acquainted.

As it turned out, Bobbie and William also lived close to each other. A beautiful, deep bond of friendship developed between the two, which eventually blossomed into a true and lasting love. Loren was not able to return to his acting career, so he decided to reside in Pomona where he and Bobbie could always remain together as a couple.

Later, Bobbie Ruth was honored by the Casa Colina Rehabilitation Center with an "Employee of the Year" award. It was quite an elaborate event, attended by eight hundred friends and supporters. Bobbie arrived at the banquet in a limo, with local media close by to cover the event. When her movie star fiancé escorted her down the red carpet, she realized that faith and reality had collided at *exactly that moment in time*!

Thirty-four years later, Bobbie and Loren still continue to share their wonderful bond of love, joy, and happiness.

JoAnn Fitzgibbons *is a native of Georgia who moved to Upland, California, in 1970. She has enjoyed a worldwide career as a design consultant for corporations, television, and beauty pageants, and owned and operated Fitzgibbons Color & Fashion Center for thirty years.* *BHShopgirl11@aol.com*

Dancing the Irish Way

by Terry Lee

About twenty-five years ago, I had a dream in my heart to carry on the tradition of ceili (kay-lee) dancing in California where I lived with my husband and three children. My daughter, Erin, was ten years old at the time and becoming a ceili dancer. Her involvement and participation helped inspire a deep desire within me to preserve this wonderful tradition and keep it alive because of all the pleasure and delight it brings to all who join in. Irish dancing is a wonderful example of how good music, dancing, and fun can bring people together in a magical spirit of gaiety and exhilaration.

Irish dance covers a group of traditional dance forms originating in Ireland, which include social dance and performance dance. Social dances can be divided further into ceili and set dancing. Set dances have been popular in Ireland for more than one hundred fifty years; they are quadrilles danced by four couples arranged in a square, whereas ceili dances are danced by varied formations of couples with two to sixteen people.

I was born in Monaghan, raised in Donegal in Ireland during World War II, and introduced to set dancing in Miltown, Malbay, Ireland. Needless to say, there was little money in those days for dance lessons, yet we somehow managed two pence once in a while during the 1940s to dance in Muff Hall, a popular social center. It was there that my love for Irish music and dancing was born and cultivated.

Once we moved to Redlands, a small town in southern California, I was lucky enough to track down the name of a teacher of Irish dance, but he lived in Canada. His name was Ron Plummer, a seven-time world champion Irish dancer. I begged him to travel the distance to Redlands to teach the tradition and finally succeeded in persuading him. But, mind you, it was hard times, as I had to drive the sixty miles to Los Angeles International Airport to pick him up, put him up, plus guarantee him twenty dancers in order to make it worth his while.

Since then, for the last three decades, I've enjoyed opening my home each week to host Irish dancing fun for family and friends. Seeing everyone enjoy themselves fills my heart with joy. Besides which, we get a good healthy workout. We share lots of laughter, merriment, and good-natured cheering as the crowd gradually becomes spirited and lively. Because some dance numbers are long and vigorous, they wear us down, leaving us exhausted and eager for a cup of tea and a biscuit. Then, while taking a short break, we always love to share the latest jokes of the week.

Although I could easily retire today, I continue to enjoy working as a registered nurse by day and hosting the high-energy ceili and set dances, which we've all come to refer to as "Irish aerobics," by night. Even after all these years, I'm all smiles when our group meets at my house each week. The dancers range in age from thirty-seven to seventy-nine, are from all walks of life and have diverse social and business backgrounds, most with no Irish heritage, but with a great sense of Irish spirit in their hearts and feet.

About a dozen of our members have started playing instruments together to form the "Ceili House Band." In fact, they've become quite popular throughout southern California and are often joined by other musicians when they perform at other functions. In past years, many of our members have even made it to dance workshops at Scoil Samhraidh Willie Clancy Week in Miltown Malbay, Ireland. Clancy was a famous step dancer and uilleann piper noted throughout Ireland. Hence, our members always return with the spirit of set dancing, which, in turn, inspires maximum enjoyment from our dancers.

Enthusiastic members who never miss a beat when the music begins are Mickey, Rita, Inessa, Erin, Bernie, Margo, Jan (author/editor of this book), David, Shirley, Kathy, Karla, Myriah, Caroline, Jolene, Jonathan, plus Susan, who will dance forever in our memories. Since many of us live on Fulbright Avenue, one day Jan christened us "The Fulbright Floosies."

I am happy to say that my dream not only came true, but year after year, it continues to flourish. Dancers love it and keep coming back for more. May our Irish welcome mat never wear out!

Teresa Lee was born in Ireland and educated in England. She became a registered nurse in 1960, and at seventy-five is still working. Terry volunteers at many jobs, including the Citizen Volunteer Patrol, Meals-on-Wheels, and the San Bernardino County Museum. She enjoys reading, gardening, and playing bridge. ptkeslee@verizon.net

About Whoopi Goldberg

Courtesy of Celebrity Short Stories, Inc.

Whoopi Goldberg is an icon, a national treasure. Ever since her gripping portrayal of Celie Johnson in *The Color Purple,* most people have loved everything she has done, including her current participation on *The View.* Her ability to be one of the funniest talents in the business, as well as to play dramatic roles superbly, is a stellar accomplishment. But as with many celebrities, life was not always so perfect for her.

Whoopi was born Caryn Elaine Johnson on November 13, 1955, in New York City. She dropped out of high school with a drug problem and took drug counseling in order to kick the habit. She has been divorced three times and has one daughter.

In the early years, Whoopi accepted small roles in Broadway productions while supporting herself working at a funeral home or as a bricklayer. She later moved to Los Angeles to hone her stand-up comedian skills. After her first major role in *The Color Purple,* she appeared in *Ghost,* for which she won an Oscar, and *Sister Act,* during which she performed songs herself. In addition to the Oscar win, Whoopi has won a Tony, Emmy, and Grammy, and was the first woman to host an Academy Awards ceremony on her own.

Whoopi is quoted as saying, "Nobody ever encouraged me in this business. I encouraged myself. I was a very dull and shy child. I was the last person you would expect to be a success in this business. But I always felt if I kept going, something would happen.

"I fear waking up one morning and finding out that my life was for nothing. We're here for a reason. I believe a bit of the reason is to throw little torches out to lead people through the dark."

Whoopi's social consciousness and charity work are remarkable. Since 1986, she has been hosting Comic Relief Specials to help people in need, and often hosts alongside such famous comedians and friends as Robin Williams and Billy Crystal. She also dedicates valuable time and energy to UNICEF, where she participates in fund-raising events and media interviews to raise awareness. In 2003, UNICEF named her a Good Will Ambassador. Whoopi Goldberg is not afraid to speak out for important causes and is recognized as a continuing voice for social justice.

Reprinted with the kind permission of **Celebrity Short Stories. www. celebrityshortstories.com**

A Gift to Remember

by Ruth Elvin

I can't begin to tell you how very much we loved and appreciated our father. His family meant the world to him, and he to us. I'll never forget how, when I was eleven years old, our country was still in a depression and work was difficult to find. My dad would accept any work anywhere just to support his family; he was a proud man.

I had a girlfriend whose father always had a steady job with the telephone company. I thought of them as being very rich because she owned a beautiful bike, all shiny and new! My dad must have overheard me talking about it and hearing me wish I could have one too. But there was no way we could afford one.

Well, it wasn't long until Christmas and without telling anyone why, my dad started spending his evenings out in the shed behind the house. What we didn't know was that he had gone to the junkyard to gather discarded wheels, chains, handlebars, and assorted bits and pieces of old bicycles.

After work, and well into the night, he cleaned, scraped, sanded, painted, screwed, and padded until he had put together a wonderful surprise Christmas present for me. A real honest-to-goodness bike!

Of course, it wasn't exactly fancy like my friend's bike. Mine was made of skinny tubing painted yellow and green, and it was a boy's bike too. But the love my dad put into it and the proud smile on his face Christmas morning when I saw it for the first time will always bring a tear to my eye.

I know that my father's true character was evident in the love and devotion he gave to our family. Many of the lessons learned from him have been valuable to me my whole life long.

Ruth Elvin, *at eighty-seven, continues to pursue life with enthusiasm. She is a licensed pilot, former gift shop owner, kindergarten teacher, author-illustrator of children's books, and mother of three. She attends a discussion group on Socrates and loves exploring life. (805) 467-3669*

Chapter 10:
HELPING HANDS,
HOPEFUL HEARTS

Seventy-Five Cents, Exact Change

by Dorothy E. Demke

In February 2002, I visited New York City, my hometown. Several members of my family still live there, so what better place could there be for us to hold a family reunion? The weather was unseasonably warm on the night when my brother, his wife, several cousins, and I all arrived at a performance of the Saint Cecilia Chorus. We were excited and feeling ever so proud because the choral conductor was none other than our ninety-year-old cousin, who had invited us to a rehearsal for an upcoming concert at Carnegie Hall.

The location was a church on Fifth Avenue across from Central Park. When we entered the building, we scarcely needed our winter coats, but when we left the building following the performance we discovered it was terribly cold and the wind that blew across the park nearly knocked us off our feet. We needed to take a cross-town bus through the park in order to get back home. By the time we had walked to the bus stop, our noses were already red, and our eyes, ears, and noses felt as though they had frozen.

It was then that I discovered I had no change. Bus fare *must* be paid by token or coins—no bills; half-price for elders was seventy-five cents. My group dug into their pockets and came up with two quarters, two dimes, and a nickel, which I gratefully clutched with my frigid fingers. Three of us were taking the bus, but I accidentally got separated from my companions and climbed aboard a moment later. We happened to be on an articulated bus, one that is two full-sized vehicles joined together by a sort of accordion in the middle. My group had already reached the back of the second bus by the time I even made it to the coin box.

I dropped my two quarters, two dimes, and nickel into the coin box and started to move along. "That's only sixty-five cents," came the stern voice of the driver. "No," I said, "I put in seventy-five." He pointed to the number, which had only registered sixty-five. By now, my family was out of range of my voice and engaged in their own conversations. Visions of my freezing to death in the park were starting. This driver was determined to put me out into the cold, actually seeming to relish the idea.

"Here, honey." Who was that? I turned to see a woman about three rows back. She was dressed in a strange assortment of ragged clothing and surrounded by plastic bags—literally a bag woman. "Here, honey," she repeated as she held out a quarter. I hesitated; how could I accept money from this poor, homeless person?

"Here," she said, still holding out the quarter to me. I took it. I took money from a kind lady who could have used it for something she badly needed! Dropping the coin into the box, I started back.

When I reached the woman, who was now smiling warmly, I tried to give her a dollar. "No, honey, I don't want it. Save it for someone who needs it," she said.

Dorothy E. Demke (*posthumously*) *grew up in New York City, where she developed a love for the visual and performing arts and studied dance. Dorothy and her husband transformed a failing bakery in Claremont, California, into an award-winning success known for its "real" butter, eggs, and flour, plus the early introduction of the croissant.*

Pray for Alice!

by Kathy May

Several family members and I had flown to Washington, D.C., to attend the burial of my brother at Arlington National Cemetery. Following that very special day of honor and remembrance, we decided we wanted to spend a couple of days sightseeing and enjoying the many points of interest that Washington has to offer. So we all purchased tickets for one of those many bus tours that allow you to hop on and off at any one of thirty-some sightseeing stops.

Just as we were boarding the bus at one of these many stops, the female bus driver unexpectedly grabbed my arm and gently pulled me back to her. "Oh, I so much want to *be* like you," she exclaimed, "but I don't have the courage! I *look* like you but just can't bring myself to do what you do." She was referencing the fact that I am a bald woman from cancer treatment and have chosen *not* to wear a wig. Just as I had lost my hair, underneath her wig she was also bald.

She added that she had recently married and that her husband had lovingly offered to shave off his hair in support of her. But her main worry was that she might not be able to withstand the stares of others, and that her coworkers might make fun of her.

Well, of course I was quick to encourage her to follow her personal desire. So in that special moment, I said, "You can do it!" Then she asked if I would please pray for her. "Of course!" I quickly answered. "What's your name?" "Alice," she replied. So I promised Alice that I would pray she would be given all the courage she needed.

We continued to ride along on Alice's bus and when we eventually reached our destination, I hurried to the front, gave Alice a big hug, and reminded her once again that I'd be praying for her. And I have been doing so ever since.

I have shared this story with many others and they've also joined me in praying for Alice. I only wish I had some way of knowing how she's doing. But God knows. So in the meantime . . . PRAY FOR ALICE!

Kathy May *is a sixty-year-old retired mother of two and is also a grandmother. She is involved in a variety of church activities, plus other interests that include singing, sewing, reading, and sports.*

Locked Inside

by Ruth Rosenthal

I drove much too fast to the psychiatric hospital, feeling burdened by anxiety over wanting to be of help but not knowing exactly what to do once I got there. Though the volunteer coordinator had briefed me, let's face it, I had no training in this field. The patients I'd be visiting were sometimes known to smash windows, break furniture, and attack each other!

My own daughter had been a patient there briefly when she was eighteen. Then Lanie's mental anguish became too much for us to handle. Now I didn't even know where Lanie was; she hadn't called in months. And whenever she did call, she just wanted me to know that she was okay, but would never tell me exactly where she was.

I pulled into the parking lot. What am I doing here? I thought. I mentally berated and scolded myself. Though I'd felt compelled to volunteer my time, I nevertheless felt inept, not knowing exactly what I'd say or do.

I got out of the car, and once inside, the volunteer coordinator greeted me warmly. "I'll take you there myself," she said, smiling. We walked down long, narrow hallways that felt disquieting, just like all the other psychiatric hospitals I'd seen. A sweet, acrid smell lingered, the same odor I remembered from visiting Lanie in other hospitals.

"There is one young man here—Tom. Be especially careful of him," the woman warned, leading the way to a large day room that was almost devoid of furniture. Bars blocked light from coming through the windows.

"How long has he been here?"

"One year next week."

My throat tightened as the heavy door was opened for me.

"That's him," she said, pointing. "Do be careful. Don't ever turn your back to him."

I was told that I would be locked in the room with the others. The ominous high ceiling and gray aura reminded me of the movie *Snake Pit.*

Several men hung around, seeming not to notice me, except for Tom. I sat down on a bench along the wall, remembering the warning given me and keeping my eyes on the movement of everyone, especially Tom. He looked up at the newly replaced windowpanes. I wondered if he were thinking of smashing a chair into them again.

Tom turned slowly and looked at me again. I sat quietly on the hard wooden bench to his right. As he walked toward me, fear rose in my throat. I thought, Oh, my God, what have I gotten myself into?

Then Tom stopped and stood in front of me. I looked up at his long, thin face and said, "Hi." No answer. I was a fragile fawn, waiting. Frozen. Then Tom sat down beside me and we examined each other with serious eyes.

"My name is Ruth," I ventured.

Tom sat still. He didn't take his eyes from my face. His eyes seemed to ask why I had come, so I answered, "I came here to visit, to see you and anyone else who would like a visit."

His silence couldn't hide his apparent intelligence. I wondered if Tom threw his food around as he did the chairs. He moved closer. I noticed his shabby, baggy brown pants as he pressed his hot, bony left leg against mine.

"Don't move," I thought, not letting down my guard for a second. "If I don't move, everything will be all right." I listened to the thoughts that rushed to me, although I didn't know where they came from.

I smiled at Tom. I hope he doesn't think I'm flirting, I thought, constantly aware of his leg against mine. I spoke whatever came to me, making light conversation, but never daring to look away or to move.

Tom lifted my right hand. I watched, almost as if I were looking through a window and seeing Tom with another person. He smiled. I let him hold my hand. He wasn't holding it like a lover. He was studying it, like an artist who was gaining perspective before painting.

"Look," he said, with pleasure in his voice. I had been so involved with my emotions that I didn't feel Tom guide my hand next to his. "Look at our rings," he said.

I looked down at the silver ring on Tom's hand. His had an intricate design carved in it, the same design on my ring. Tom laughed in delight for a moment, then caught himself and resumed his quiet, sober demeanor. Our legs, still touching, seemed to vibrate together and generate a heat that encompassed my entire being. Tom smiled, "You felt it too, didn't you?" he asked. "Yes," I answered with surprise. "That's because you understand me," he added. "Thank you for that."

When it was time to leave, I stood up and spoke. "I'll come back; I promise." Then an attendant on the other side of the door unlocked it for me.

I drove home in the slow lane, this time not in any hurry whatsoever, trying to digest what had just occurred. A few days later, my contact person at the hospital phoned. "How did you do it?" she asked.

"Do what?" I responded, sounding puzzled.

"I can't believe it's the same Tom. When he first came here, Ruth, all he did was suck on baby bottles. Then he progressed to violent behavior. But he never, ever said a word until your visit. Now he talks to everyone."

"Thank you for telling me."

I knew what had helped Tom. The next time Lanie calls, I thought, I'll be ready.

Ruth Rosenthal *established a poetry group for psychiatric patients at Marin General Hospital in California, where amazing changes were noted in patients who expressed their deepest feelings and discovered their hidden joys. Ruth has authored* Like Fallen Snow, *a memoir in poems, and* Maybe Shirts are Easier: A Path Back to Life, *about a widow's grief. (559) 240-5533*

The Block Party

by Dr. Carolyn Bohler

Soon after our family moved into our new neighborhood in Dayton, Ohio, we learned that an annual "block party" was held on our street each summer. Our street was just one block long, so it was fairly easy to define who our neighbors were, and everyone on the block was invited to attend this traditional celebration. Then, after several years of participating and sharing our potluck dishes, those of us attending realized that only *half* the block was ever represented, even though we always made certain that each family was invited, with written invitations placed at everyone's door.

Approximately eighteen families lived on that block. Most of us living on one end of the street were European Americans, and most on the other end were African Americans. But the only families who ever attended our block parties were white. And the more we white folks got to know each other, the easier it became for us to say *they* are invited, *they* just aren't coming, etc. Yet it was really our sincere desire to have everyone attend.

Then one year, we decided we'd ask our children to be in charge. Well, it wasn't long before the children not only succeeded in contacting all the kids on the block and making sure they knew all the details of the party, but that plenty of fun races, games, and activities were organized and planned, as well. And as if that wasn't enough, they also made certain that it was far more than the usual casseroles that were assigned and served.

And yes, the year that the children took charge was the year that the *whole block* turned out! Only then did we all finally get to know each other at last. That day marked the beginning of many beautiful new friendships for everyone. Oh, the brainpower and "know-how" of children! Their solutions are often the easiest and the best.

Dr. Carolyn Stahl Bohler *is lead pastor of First United Methodist Church, Redlands, California. She is the mother of two and author of six books, including* God the *What?* What Our Metaphors for God Reveal About Our Beliefs in God. *She was professor of pastoral theology and counseling at United Theological Seminary in Dayton, Ohio for twenty-one years.* carolynbohler@redlandsfirstchurch.org

The Helping Hand

by Bobbie F. Henry

Many years ago, before the law was established that all handicapped children were entitled to receive an appropriate education, I cofounded a multiple handicapped program in my hometown in Oregon. My cofounder was a mother of a child with cerebral palsy, as was I. At the time, my son had already undergone two surgeries and continued to need further assistance.

She and I decided to hold a public meeting and to invite parents of other handicapped children to join us in planning an educational program for our special kids. The editor of our small town newspaper readily agreed to publicize the meeting at no charge to us. When the day of the meeting finally arrived we were stunned by the wonderful response and unexpected turnout, almost as if parents of all types of handicapped kids appeared from "out of the woodwork." Soon, we were introduced to a politician who influenced one of the schools to provide two classrooms, teachers, and even special buses to transport the children. Miracles!

I became an assistant to the speech therapist and helped in as many ways as I could. I remember that when working with one special little boy, we wore golf score gadgets on our wrists. We used them to count his screams, for he did not talk. He would only vocalize screams—as many as two hundred times a day. I worked with him daily and one day he finally spoke. Imagine my thrill when his first word was my name, *Bobbie*! After that, he screamed no more, but called my name out repeatedly. I was also able to teach him words, to count numbers, and to read ABCs.

It was a wondrous time in my life and I'm blessed to have countless rich memories of the many loveable children I worked with. I was presented a medal by the city for my contribution to this program, but the best reward was not the medal. It was the love I received from all the beautiful handicapped children, their teachers, and parents.

Later, my oldest son was diagnosed with a rare type of cancer, Burkitt's lymphoma. He was one of only six people in the world to have it at that time, and was believed to be only the second person to survive it. Since there was no support group for families of cancer patients at the time, out of my need for emotional support and to help meet the needs of others, I founded "Cancer—We Care." Once again, it was with the help of a newspaper editor and people who joined the care group.

The following poem was written for me by one of my cancer patients who died in my arms. I hold it as the greatest tribute and honor I've ever received and cherish the original that he sent me, written in his shaky handwriting.

The Helping Hand
by Jess Ely

Every day's a happy day
when Bobbie comes to town,
Always helping someone
for many miles around.

She's always very helpful,
she really has a care.
When a helping hand is needed,
Bobbie Henry's always there.

No matter what their need is,
I've heard so many say,
Always there to cheer them

for a brighter day.

Everyone is smiling
just to hear her name,
Does her work completely
and never does complain.

Has a smile for everyone
as she hurries on her way,
Filling hearts with sunshine
to brighten up their day.

We need more Bobbie Henrys
in this world we're living in.
People seem so busy
in this old world of sin.

When her days are over
and the battle is won,
There awaits a crown of glory
beyond the rising sun.
In the golden mansion
away beyond the sky
Where there are no cancer victims
and people never die.

Bobbie F. Henry *is an eighty-three-year-old widow who has been honored with the "Citizen of the Year" award. She is an animal lover—with fifty-two pets so far—cancer caregiver, and founder of a multiple handicapped program in Oregon. As the mother of eight children, she now boasts thirty-seven great grandchildren! (909) 948-9018*

Chapter 11:
MEMORABLE MEMORIALS

You Gotta Laugh!

by Mavis Mathews

I t was another cold day with patches of rain on the Mendocino Coast of California. I had just finished a one o'clock class but still had some time to kill while in town, so impulsively I decided to go to the gym.

Then I noticed that there was a fabric store in the same shopping center, so I made a quick U-turn, pulled up near the door, and went inside. A lovely young woman offered to help me.

Two years earlier, when I turned eighty and was anticipating hip surgery, I had decided I'd better make some preparations just in case I died as a result of the operation. So for the very first time, I had a will drawn up to spare my heirs time, money, a lot of frustration—and maybe sanity. I purchased *A Graceful Farewell: Putting Your Affairs in Order,* by Maggie Watson, and proceeded to fill in the needed information. I also decided to check out the local crematorium to gather information about arrangements, all of which forced me to consider what I would wear for my cremation. After giving it considerable thought, I felt strongly that my shroud should be a plain and simple white gown. I would make it myself.

So now here I was, finally asking a clerk to please show me what was available in 100 percent white cotton fabric (synthetics don't burn cleanly). She nodded pleasantly and led me to a section where she reached for three bolts of fabric in white cotton. We selected the one that was the least sheer. Next, she directed me to the patterns. Since there wasn't a vast selection of available patterns—and to my disappointment, no caftan pattern at all—I spent a long time trying to figure out which one would work best. I finally settled on a long dress pattern.

Next, this lovely clerk helped me determine exactly how much fabric would be needed, then began measuring and cutting four yards for me. As she did this, she attempted to make friendly, light-hearted conversation, and—so help me, this is what she asked—"So . . . are you going to some nice warm place where you can wear this?"

Had there not been lots of other people shopping in the store at the time, I might have told her the truth. But instead, I quickly replied, *"Yeah . . . I sure am. I'm going straight to hell!"*

Mavis Mathews *tried to retire upon turning sixty-five twenty years ago, but her excessive energy won't let her quit. She is the author of* Getting Lucky at Eighty *and still remains active as a realtor. She lives in Mendocino Coast, CA, and enjoyed a long career that included teaching, radio, television, and newspaper work.* http://lifeaftereighty.wordpress. com *or* mavis@mcn.org

A Living Memorial

by Shirley Huston

Several months following the death of my husband, Dyer, I realized that I would soon be nearing my seventy-fifth birthday. This year, it was my deepest wish to pull out all stops and to celebrate my blessed life while surrounded by my beautiful family. And so I decided to host a family reunion and treat all of my loved ones to a lavish fun-filled getaway weekend in scenic Palm Desert, California.

First, I invited our six beloved children and spouses (well, five spouses and one fiancée), six grandchildren, plus my nephew and his wife, to my seventy-fifth birthday bash. Oh, what fun! The more deeply involved I got in making the arrangements, the more excited I became; I knew that my dear Dyer would have thoroughly loved and enjoyed every single minute of the planning and preparation along with me.

The accommodations I had reserved for each family were plush. I had rented three gorgeous three-bedroom adjoining condos, each with comfy sofa beds, large kitchens, plus Jacuzzi hot tubs on their patios. In addition, there were tennis courts, an Olympic-sized swimming pool, jogging trails, and a golf course available for everyone's enjoyment throughout our three-day stay. But as it turned out—and much to my delight—most of our hours were spent enjoying each other's company, sharing memories, and, of course, eating.

As each family arrived on the scene, I handed them the key to their assigned condo, a copy of our informal social and recreational agenda, plus menus for each day. Yes, it had been my pleasure to do all the food shopping in advance, as well as some cooking and planning of our buffet settings. After all, this was a special occasion, wasn't it? So everything seemed worthy of an extra special touch.

There was only one "house rule" I asked everyone to observe—to please be present for every evening meal and family get-together afterwards. Otherwise, they were completely free and on their own. To my delight, however, everyone seemed to enjoy huddling together, congregating in and around my condo, while laughing, talking, reminiscing, sharing wine, champagne, and special memories—some of which were news to me. (I honestly never knew that two of my "angelic" boys had shot their BB guns off at our neighbor's garbage can!)

Then on our final evening together, as we were enjoying the last of my birthday cake, I asked the group if they recalled the many loving statements people had made at "Grand Dyer's" memorial service. Once I saw them nodding and smiling, I said I only wished that *he* had been able to hear his family, friends, and coworkers speak so lovingly about the impact he'd had on their lives.

It was then that I announced my one remaining birthday wish.

My wish was this. I asked if they would please use their imagination and pretend that they were attending a memorial service for me. *Right now!* And that they were being invited to say a few words about what I'd meant to them during my lifetime. Even though I made it perfectly clear that *I fully intended to be around for many, many more years!*

But this year for my birthday, all I wanted was to watch their dear faces and hear their voices as they spoke about their mom, grandmom, aunt, and friend. As it turned out, the events of that night turned out to be an even more "memorable memorial" than I could ever have imagined. Yes, my loving family didn't disappoint me, but gifted me with laughter, tears, and a truly "Happy Birthday"!

I believe that we seniors really need to hear all the good things people feel about us *while we're still alive to enjoy all the love!* If you agree, then why not have a "memorable memorial" party with your family and friends? I found mine to be uplifting, energizing, and most unforgettable.

Shirley Huston *is a retired marketing executive who "unretired" to serve as executive director of a trade association for thirteen years. She has written a newspaper column, plus numerous media and corporate commercials and promotional materials. Shirley is a literary agent and editor for several budding authors. shuston.litagent@verizon.net*

Unforgettable Moments

by Jeanie Lowry

After thirty-six years of marriage, my wonderful husband, Paul, was diagnosed with Alzheimer's disease. Fortunately, however, he wasn't subjected to a long period of suffering; he passed away just two years later at the age of eighty-three. In preparation for his memorial service, I searched my mind trying to recall at least one light-hearted, amusing, but cherished anecdote related to his affliction that I could share with others. I finally chose the following humorous reminiscence to relay to the 210 people who attended his service.

On rare but wonderful evenings when we found ourselves at home, Paul would sit in his wingback chair. I would toss a pillow on the floor in front of him, then lean back between his knees and watch television. Paul would then rub my shoulders, and stroke and play with my hair for long periods of time. I just loved it! But eventually his hands and arms would tire so he'd stop to rest. At that point, I'd simply turn around and say, "Honey, please don't stop; you just began." It always worked! And he would immediately begin the process all over again—for hours on end!

Jeanie Lowry is a seventy-one-old widow and retired kindergarten teacher who lives and loves every second of every day. She is now a special events director credited with developing creative settings and themes. She loves tending her "Purple Paradise" garden, golfing, and cruising the Newport Harbor in her award-winning tugboat "Tug O' My Heart."

The Builder

by Elaine Roberts

"He was a *man's* man, a Mr. Fix-it, a sportsman . . ."
"No, I don't think so. He was a *woman's* man, a good listener, a fabulous dancer . . ."

"No, he was a *grandfather* who asked hard—sometimes embarrassing—questions, a loving friend, a beloved uncle, and a man who had an opinion about everything and shared it whether you wanted to hear it or not . . ."

There we were, all assembled on our first night together in a remote village in Honduras where we'd all come as volunteers to help build a computer center and an extra classroom to honor the life of Jack Allen. Each of us spoke of our special connection to Jack and why we were there. Now we were memorializing him, each in our own way, and learning that Jack encompassed *all* of the personal tributes that were mentioned.

It first began in 2001 when Jack was seventy-seven. It was his first visit to Central America, where he'd gone to assist a small Nicaraguan village of twenty families in building a community wash house. Until then, the women of the village had to travel quite a distance to wash their clothes in the river where the animals walked and drank. The wash house was a vast improvement, for it consisted of four washing stations and two cubicles with doors. The cubicles were called showers, and even though they had no running water yet, they provided privacy for people to wash themselves. Cold running water was available in the washing stations, along with concrete wash tubs and scrub boards.

Jack had become quickly hooked, and returned to Central America as a volunteer five more times until his death at age eighty-three. Sometimes he assisted a family in building a better home or helped a village build a community center. Once, he took part in the construction of a women's agricultural cooperative in Guatemala.

Volunteering was Jack's way of expressing solidarity with people who were struggling to make a better life for themselves. It was a way for him to live out his belief that we're all connected, and to manifest the Unitarian principle of affirming world community with justice, equity, and peace for all. Jack was building world community one cement block at a time. The memorial fund set up when he died provided the funds, and we lovingly provided the "grunt work" to make the computer center become a reality.

Jack was a teacher, so he'd be pleased and happy to know that his living legacy in Honduras is a computer center and a classroom that will continue to bless the lives of many.

Elaine Roberts *is a Canadian Unitarian Universalist, a storyteller, and activist who has spent time in Central America volunteering with World Accord, a Canadian nongovernmental organization (NGO). lainey@telus.net*

Where Lilies Grow

by Dawn Huntley Spitz

Not every singer can boast of having a police car escort her to her own performance. Nor is every writer honored to have her work cast in bronze and publicly displayed. Just after turning seventy, however, I had the distinct joy and pleasure of experiencing both.

To be perfectly candid, the police didn't exactly "escort" me. If the truth be fully told, an officer was closely following our car in order to issue us a speeding ticket. My husband and I were passengers who were riding with my college roommate and her husband, our driver, en route to our fiftieth reunion memorial service at Skidmore College. At my frantic pleading, the officer had reluctantly, but kindly, consented to allow us to at least reach our destination because it was an important event that I was participating in.

And so we arrived at the very last minute, the police in tow. Nonetheless, I could see that our waiting classmates were impressed by our unorthodox entrance.

The service included a memorial ceremony in which our class was dedicating a lovely lily garden in front of the student center to honor our classmates who had died. As a former music major, I was invited to sing at the service. This was especially meaningful to me because the garden was a tribute to my music composition professor, Stanley Saxton, faculty emeritus. The cultivation of the special lilies we were planting had been his hobby, which had won him worldwide recognition.

Wanting to sing something appropriate for this occasion, as well as to honor Mr. Saxton, I had written a musical prayer titled "Where

Lilies Grow." And so as we, the Class of 1952, now stood in silence on that beautiful May afternoon in Saratoga Springs, New York, with the foothills of the Adirondacks highlighted by a brilliant sunset, the names of our deceased classmates were read aloud by our class president. Though it was difficult to hold back tears upon hearing the names of some of our beloved college friends, I was grateful to have the opportunity to pay them tribute with my own words and music.

Five years later, at our fifty-fifth reunion memorial service, once again I was invited to sing. This time, I stood beside a small granite monument containing a bronze plaque. On it was engraved the first verse of my composition, "Where Lilies Grow." My class had chosen those words to be preserved for all time. A framed and illustrated copy of the entire poem now hangs in the Skidmore alumni office:

> *Bless this place where lilies grow*
> *For those we knew so long ago.*
> *Who since have reached their journey's end.*
> *We mourn each lost, beloved friend.*

It is never too late to use one's talents in a meaningful way.

Dawn Huntley Spitz, *seventy-nine, is a teacher, performer, member of the National League of American Pen Woman, and past president of the Palm Springs, California Writers' Guild. She serves as a volunteer for her college, church, as well as for nursing homes. dawnlspitz@aol.com*

Chapter 12:
NEVER TOO LATE

Back to Space

by John Glenn

I couldn't believe what was happening. "What in the world is going on?" I kept asking Annie.

NASA's announcement on January 16 that I would join the crew of the space shuttle *Discovery* on a mission dubbed STS-95 set off a hubbub that simply wouldn't die down. It was reminiscent of the beginnings of the Mercury program. We'd known there would be some attention, but we expected it to ease off in a week or two. We were wrong.

Annie came with me almost every time I went to Houston. She sat in on my classes, observed my training, and learned along with me. She also talked to the scientists who were conducting the aging studies. As time went on, the two of us tried to analyze what kept the media and the public so interested in my return to space at age seventy-seven.

Annie told me it was because people in America needed somebody to look up to. There was another factor, too. People my age weren't really expected to do much. Even when older individuals had higher expectations than that, society tended to take a dim view. The old folks should be slowing down, not trying to act as if they were young. The general idea was for them to stand aside and get out of the way. And that's what too many people did, just sat around like couch potatoes and waited out their years. The idea of an ancient guy like me going into outer space was exhilarating.

The truth is, the old stereotypes no longer fit, if ever they did. Older people are increasingly active. My scheduled return to space helped bring this trend into the open. Older people were gratified at the evidence that they remained important.

When I said during a television appearance that older people have just as many dreams and ambitions as anybody else and that they should continue to pursue them, I got an outpouring of supportive letters and e-mails. The elderly were agreeing with me wholeheartedly and eloquently.

One day at Houston Intercontinental Airport, a couple about my age stopped me. The man said, "I just wanted to tell you that you've changed my life."

"How's that?" I asked.

"All my life, ever since I was a boy, I was fascinated with Mount Kilimanjaro. I read about it, and I wanted to climb it. Then I got married, and we had kids, and I just kept putting it off. Then my wife told me I was too old." He glanced at his wife, who was laughing and rolling her eyes. "But now I've been telling her that if John Glenn can go back into space at seventy-seven, I can climb Mount Kilimanjaro, and we've got tickets to Africa next month."

"That's great," I said, and it was.

More than anything, I think the excitement surrounding my return to space was due to that redefinition of what people could expect of the elderly, and what the elderly could expect of themselves.

From *John Glenn, A Memoir* by John Glenn and Nick Taylor, copyright © 1999 by John Glenn. Used by permission of Bantam Books, a division of Random House, Inc.

John Glenn *served as a Marine Corps fighter pilot, astronaut, and U.S. senator. In 1962, he became the first American to orbit the earth and returned to space for a second flight at age 77 to provide valuable research on the effects of spaceflight upon the elderly. He has been awarded numerous medals, decorations, and commendations for meritorious achievement.*

Young at Heart

by Barbara J. Broton

I share my story in hopes of offering inspiration to seniors who may believe that companionship and good times are over for them. It's not necessarily true! After enjoying a successful, loving marriage for forty years, my husband died. Afterwards, bereft of all hope for the future, I recall how I had pretty much resigned myself to living a life that would be limited to familiar habits, old friends, lonely days, and empty nights. Never once did I dare imagine that I could meet someone new to share my life with again!

Call it Kismet, call it fate, but . . .

It just so happened that there were two young ladies with playful matchmaking ideas who felt strongly that Gaylen and I should be introduced to each other. Both girls worked in the office of our mutual physician. So, after two months had gone by, with he and I just missing each another at appointments, their persistence finally paid off and Gaylen and I met at last. Our introduction was followed by a lovely long telephone conversation, after which I just "coincidentally" showed up exactly where I knew he'd be the next day. You see, he worked part-time as a courier for the same bank where I happened to have an account.

Although we discovered that we only lived six miles apart, we also discovered that we came from vastly different backgrounds, as well as different parts of the country. Gaylen was born and raised in the state of Washington, where he'd lived his entire life. I'd lived in many states—Maryland, Illinois, Florida, North Carolina, and California—before moving to Washington fifteen years earlier.

And yet it was uncanny when we soon realized how much we had in common, including our previous employment in banking, the building industry, even our political beliefs. We also quickly discovered so many similar interests. At the top of the list was our passionate love of music—specifically Frank Sinatra, whom we each consider to be the greatest all-time pop singer and interpreter of lyrics ever. Imagine our surprise and astonishment when we realized that our CD collections were nearly identical! In fact, between us we have a very extensive, impressive library.

Ever since our first meeting, we've continued to enjoy getting to know each other better and better. We find joy and pleasure in one another's company and have shared memorable wine tastings, quiet dinners for two (and not-so-quiet dinners with friends), lots of traveling, listening to good music, attending local concerts, movies, and so much more.

There are many Sinatra hits that could easily apply to the two of us. Among them is the one with memorable words we've frequently echoed from one of our all-time favorites, "The Best is Yet to Come." Not to mention his other hit songs, "Young at Heart" and "The Second Time Around." My dear Gaylen and I have always treated each day as a precious gift to be savored and enjoyed.

So remember, it really is true when they say it's never too late to be "Young at Heart"!

Barbara J. Broton and Gaylen Houser's home is in Skagit Valley, Washington. They cherish their time together and have enjoyed many travels, including a memorable three-week tour of the Southwest desert. More recently, they have discovered the joys of ballroom dancing.

Where Is China Camp?

by Anthony A. Krizan

For many years now, I'd been overhearing conversations about the difficult challenges of locating China Camp, the site of an early Chinese settlement in the 1880s whose historic cabins are located somewhere in the Ansel Adams Wilderness in the Sierra Nevada Mountains of California. Packers traveling into this area often use a trail that departs from a four-wheel-drive road leading to Onion Springs. Another trail begins at Mono Hot Springs, but is a much longer distance to hike.

It was late summer when I just happened to be enjoying a relaxing week camping at Mono Hot Springs. But one afternoon, my curiosity got the best of me and I thought I just might attempt to uncover the mystery of locating China Camp the next morning.

I reasoned that if I were to leave before daybreak, maybe I could complete the loop and be back at my campsite before dark. Though it would be arduous, I planned to depart Mono, hike north toward Onion Springs Road, follow the road east past Edison Lake, locate the final four-mile trail heading south toward Mono Creek, and then return back to Mono Hot Springs.

I couldn't find anyone who'd volunteer to join me on this fourteen-mile hiking adventure. So, as it turned out, my map and compass were my only companions on this solo wilderness trek.

Eight years earlier, I had attempted this hike but the trail had deteriorated to the point of becoming untraceable. So after hours of disappointment, I had turned back hoping to complete the adventure one day in the future. This morning was the future. With the first rays of light forming over the eastern mountains, this time I hoped to succeed. However, the trails leading to the camp remained neglected, as decades of local ranchers who grazed their cattle had created many false paths.

During my first hour, Tule Lake, Mono Meadow, and Mosquito Crossing at Mono Creek disappeared under my footsteps. Eight years ago, a huge pine tree had provided a bridge to cross Mono Creek. The log was still there, a little weather beaten, but once again strong enough to support my weight.

After two hours of gaining elevation, Warm Creek came into view. I changed direction and hiked north, following the creek until it crossed a large meadow. Even in September, a few wild flowers still displayed their beautiful colors, drawing moisture from the sparkling creek. At this point, the cabins should have been visible on an elevated area to the northeast. Where were they?

Then, finally, *finally*, after eight years of mystery, there they were!

Both cabins awaited me at the east end of the meadows. One was built for living quarters and the other a bunk house barn. Even the corrals and fences surrounding the cabins were still standing, like sentries guarding this historic site. Though these structures were built more than one hundred years ago, time and weather had been patient with their existence. Maybe with a little hard labor, they could even be livable again, I thought.

I spent more than one hour photographing the rustic charm of this area, then looked for the trail leading toward the Onion Springs Road. I was in luck. But after fifteen minutes, I knew something wasn't right. This was the wrong trail!

Now I'd have to double back to the cabins and figure out another route. The map showed a trail west of my location that appeared to intersect with an old trail leading to the road. So after crossing two moraines, I located the trail and followed it for more than a quarter of a mile. But it also turned west into the interior of the valley. Again, another incorrect decision. I'd have to return to the cabins a second time!

But rather than return by my original route, I considered another game plan. Sitting down next to one of the cabins, an idea came to mind. What in this area was out of place? Then I remembered having seen a pole gate with recently cut rails, which might mean there was activity at this location and, if so, maybe the ground would reveal horseshoe prints.

Yes, after examining the ground on the opposite side, I spotted faded tracks leading up the mountain, so I quickly grabbed my pack and followed the tracks. Within ten minutes, they intersected with another trail—a lightly-traveled one, but one lacking in any human shoe prints. Instead, there were fresh bear tracks in various sizes at five separate locations. Luck had sure been with me during that hot afternoon, with no physical bear sightings for me!

Two hours later, I arrived at the Edison Lake Vermilion, took a short break, then with only four miles to go, I finally crossed the swinging bridge at Mono Creek and was back to Mono Hot Springs where I'd started from.

I did it! And yes, it was worth waiting eight years to feel the thrill, satisfaction, and accomplishment of finally having completed this wonderful adventure.

Anthony (Tony) Krizan *writes stories for his local newspaper about his thirty-plus years hiking the Sierra Nevada Mountains. He is an active member of Kiwanis, which helps serve children of the world.*

Never Too Late to Change

by Margaret (Peggy) Burnett

In 1993, I discontinued my cable television service and donated my TV to the Salvation Army. I seemed to have reached a point in life where I felt I had more important and enjoyable options, such as spending true quality time with my many grandchildren. Plus attending concerts, theater, lectures, personal enrichment college courses, and returning to the great outdoors and my "country girl" roots. In addition to these many desires, I also felt a strong yearning to immerse myself in my favorite passions: reading, photography, and travel.

One day many years later, I received the most unexpected call from a longtime dear friend who lives several hundred miles away; he said he was calling to say, "Good-bye." Six months earlier, he had been diagnosed with ocular melanoma, a rare cancer for which there is little research or medical standard of care; it was now beginning to spread. In addition, there were other worrisome medical complications and concerns. I listened compassionately while he described his months-long depression, during which he just sat in front of the television. In his words he was "not really watching, hearing, or even caring about what was on the screen."

But then a while later, he called me back. This time, it was to say he remembered that I didn't have a TV and spoke about how much he had always admired my lifestyle. As he continued talking, he shared how he'd finally come to terms with the reality and inevitability of his current situation. Then, to my surprise, he astonished me by saying that he'd not only decided to turn off his *own* TV, but that he'd also begun to take walks in the scenic semi-rural area where he lived. In fact, he was making a conscious effort to resume as many favorite activities as his health would permit, including taking his wife on a cruise!

He ended the conversation with a warm "Thank you. You've made a world of difference for me and my wife!"

As I reflect back on our conversations, many thoughts drift through my mind, but the one that stands out the most is the old, time-honored adage, "Our actions speak louder than words."

(P.S. Imagine my surprise and delight when I later received a Christmas card from him with the notation, "Let's do lunch!")

Margaret (Peggy) Burnett is a sixty-nine-year-old award-winning photographer who has raised six children. She is a former Marine sky diver and retired registered nurse who now serves as a worldwide volunteer with Earthwatch environmental and science expeditions, plus Global Volunteers humanitarian-based projects. (909) 883-3791 or P.O. Box #417, Patton, CA 92369

The Best is Yet to Come

by Joan van Ommen

When I celebrated my sixty-fifth birthday a while ago, it forced me to admit I'd been noticing some subtle signs of aging creeping up on me over the previous few years. For example, an accidental fall had left me feeling bruised and sore for months, the kind of thing that I used to recover from quickly. Plus, I felt I was losing confidence in my ability to try out something new.

Then, the first miracle occurred.

I decided to take a chance and enroll in an adult education creative writing class held at our local senior center. To my surprise and amazement, I soon realized that I not only liked it, but loved it! It was as if I'd discovered a voice inside that had always been there but had never been used. I first began by writing about true life experiences and gradually learned to embellish facts with enough detail to flesh out reality and make it more interesting. It wasn't long before words flowed easily, almost eagerly. I was on my way to writing fiction!

The next awakening was the computer. For years I'd told everyone I was *not* interested in owning one. No place to put it. Didn't need one. Then one day my son appeared on a surprise visit, burdened with boxes that he plunked down all over my desk. "A computer, Mom!" John announced. "I'm going to set it up for you and now you can learn to use it."

I stared at it for days, afraid to follow his handwritten instructions for playing solitaire. Will it explode if I do something wrong? Finally, the solution came. Return to the senior center for a beginning computer class. Amazingly, the mystery of the computer was no longer a mystery, nor was it difficult at all to figure out once I conquered my fear of trying something new. I also discovered one more thing. Once I began to challenge my mind with new information, it expanded and grew. I wasn't such a dummy anymore. No longer a Luddite!

Last miracle was the body makeover. (Well, I confess I'm still working on that.) I've always loved dancing, be it ballet, jazz, aerobics, jazzercise, line dancing—you name it. I had done it all in the past. Turning again to the senior center, this time I enrolled in a Pilates class. Wonderful, but tough. Then one day when the instructor resigned and there was no one to teach the class, I surprised the director by insisting "I can do this class." And I meant not as a follower, but a teacher. Praise the Lord, the next thing I knew I became the teacher!

So far, I've dropped ten pounds, lost one of my three chins, and have firmed the flesh on my arms. Last night while walking my dog, I noticed that my step was more sprightly, brisk, and energetic than even six months ago.

So why did all of this happen so quickly? I'd like to believe it's because I took the first step. Six months ago, I was clearly an aging woman. Now I know that the best is yet to come, and can't wait to tell my son, John, how he truly changed my life just by giving me that computer.

Could it be that Mother doesn't *always* know best?

Joan van Ommen is seventy-two. She began actively writing after retirement because "friends always told me I was good at it." In addition to teaching an exercise class for seniors, she is a part-time elementary school tutor. Among her favorite companions are cats Smokey and Chomley. (909) 798-3486, joanvanommen@hotmail.com

Finding My Place in the Desert

by Shirley Gibson

At age sixty-two, my life changed forever. Suddenly, here I was leaving my accounting and bookkeeping position of twenty years and moving nearly two thousand miles away! It all began when my friend, Jane, came to Indiana for a visit. Over lunch, she updated me on her life and mentioned that she was switching careers and quitting her job as director of an art gallery in Palm Springs, California, to become a real estate agent.

During the conversation, she mentioned that the gallery was seeking a new director, then quite unexpectedly smiled at me and asked, "With your art background, why don't you apply for the job?" It was certainly true that my background included painting and stained glass-making, but I was nevertheless shocked by her sudden suggestion. However, the idea was appealing to me and seemed to hold merit, even though I had never before lived *anywhere* but in my own hometown. Now what was I going to do?

Well, I began by making a few bold phone calls and the next thing I knew I was on a plane to Palm Springs, headed for an interview with the gallery owner! Once we met, I walked away with the job that very day, about to begin a brand new life. What a new experience this would be for me, I marveled as I returned to Indiana to prepare for my courageous move.

And so on September 11, 2004, I packed up my car with all that it would hold and left for California. Longtime friends shook their heads, wondering how I could just pick up and move across country at my age. But I was *ready* for a new experience. Four years earlier, I'd been to Palm Springs to visit my sister in a tennis tournament and knew that I loved the desert, wishing even then that I could live there. Now that dream was coming true.

I soon grew to love my new position as director of the art gallery. Holding meetings with other artists and preparing for opening events was new and exciting for me, and all the while I was enjoying the gorgeous view of mountains just outside my window. Nearly one year later, however, my job came to an end because the gallery closed. But by then I loved Palm Springs and knew I would find a way to continue to make it my home.

At first, I filled my time by playing bridge at the local senior center, and before I knew it, had met new people and made many new friends. Then one day I stopped at a local ceramic studio and learned that they needed part-time help, so I soon began working for them two days a week. It wasn't long before I had mastered enough skills about the business that I was often put in charge when the owners were gone. Besides, there was a potter's wheel in the back room. I took lessons and loved learning a creative new craft.

In the past few years, I've had time to enroll in a creative writing class, collectively publish my stories along with other classmates, and am now finding time to fulfill my lifelong dream of writing books for children. This season in life is a time of beauty, a wonderful opportunity to explore my creativity. Palm Springs is an awe-inspiring oasis in the desert. I truly believe I have found paradise in my senior years.

The Desert

by Shirley Gibson

The shifting sands slithered across the desert,
searching for what?
Crawling over rocks and seeking out crevices to hide,
it is alive with movement.
Is it running from something or just wanting change?

High above the desert, the mountains stretch upward
as if to worship an invisible God.
The sun slowly creeps over the mountain,
spreading light through the valley.
It touches the golf course as if someone
magically turned on a light switch.
The trees cast their shadows, overlapping
and mingling with one another.
A hummingbird swoops to a nearby feeder,
the first to feed, then quickly dashes away, filled.
The pool reflects the towering palm trees.
Another beautiful day awakens in the desert . . .

Shirley Gibson *is a sixty-eight-year-old artist, stained-glass maker, and writer who retired from a long career in accounting and bookkeeping. She now writes fiction for children, based on magical, mystical childhood daydreams that arouse and inspire the imagination like a magic carpet ride to another dimension. (812) 212-1220*

An Unforgettable Gift

by Joan van Ommen

Just before my mother died at the age of ninety-six in the year 2000, she was finally able to say, "I have lived in two centuries." For the last ten years or so, whenever Mom approached a birthday, she'd announce with great seriousness, "I have the feeling this is going to be my very last year." To which I would immediately smile and reply, "Of course not. You're in such good health you'll be here for a long time yet." And so she was.

Mom hated going to doctors and put her faith in vitamins instead. In fact, an entire shelf in her refrigerator door was stocked with eighteen different bottles. When she turned ninety, however, she finally conceded that she should probably make regular doctor visits for medications to strengthen and regulate her heartbeat. One doctor, who happened to be a disciple of holistic medicine, once advised, "The reason you've survived so long might be because of all those vitamins you take." And who knows? It may very well have been true.

My mother seemed very wise about how to live a stress-free life. If she didn't want to do something, she simply didn't do it. Even when I'd beg her to come join us for a holiday dinner, if she wasn't in the mood, absolutely nothing could move her. She'd simply reply, "No thank you, I'd just as soon stay home today and watch television." Or, "I'm just going to stay here and work in the yard."

I cannot ever remember Mom saying "I love you." She was extremely reticent about expressing emotions of affection, so my sister, Lois, and I grew up not saying those words either. But Lois eventually married into a family who spoke "I love you" as freely as "hello" and "good-bye," so she became accustomed to saying "Good-bye. I love you, Mother" after a visit. In time, I learned to follow Lois's lead, also saying "I love you, Mother" before leaving. But the closest I ever remember Mother replying in kind was, "Me too!"

But one day, she finally did leave us and died peacefully in her sleep. In the days following her funeral, as Lois and I were sorting through piles of paper and trivia in Mom's empty house, to our great surprise, we discovered a handwritten page in a partially-used spiral notebook. In it, she had written the following, using a heavy black marker, *"Thank you. I was blessed with two lovely daughters and I had a good life. Thank you, my darlings. I love you, Mom."*

God must have guided us to find this one hidden page because it certainly wasn't marked in any special way for us to find it. To think how easily we might have tossed out the entire notebook along with other useless trivia and never found it! Who knows when Mom had written it?

And that was the only time I ever remember Mother saying, "I love you." What a priceless, unforgettable gift!

Joan van Ommen *is seventy-two and began actively writing following retirement because "friends always told me I was good at it." In addition to teaching an exercise class for seniors, Joan is a part-time elementary school tutor. Among her favorite companions are cats Smokey and Chomley. (909) 798-3486, joanvanommen@hotmail.com*

Chapter 13:
AND SO IT GOES

The Clothes Chute

by Gloria Burke

There are moments when I longingly wish I still had a clothes chute. But I haven't had one since those early days of marriage when we lived in an old two-story house. Admittedly, there are fewer loads of laundry now, but as "eighty-something" settles in, it nevertheless becomes more difficult to carry those baskets of laundry up and down the basement stairs.

I can recall one morning in particular when my three-year-old son, Lee, watched me while I sped through my usual morning ritual of making beds and spiffing up bedrooms, then carried an armload of laundry into the bathroom. When I began dropping the clothes down the chute, a few at a time in anticipation of laundering them later, Lee suddenly reacted quite tearfully, "Mommy, why do you throw my clothes away every day?"

Of course, it had never occurred to me that it certainly did look as if I were throwing his clothes away. "But that's not what I'm doing, honey," I replied. Then, not wanting to miss a teachable moment, I said, "Come on now, come with me. I'll show you what happens after Mommy throws dirty clothes down the chute."

Yes, I do remember the luxury of having that clothes chute!

Even though I now live on one floor, I'd give anything if I could simply drop my laundry down a chute instead of having to carry several basket loads of soiled clothes down to the basement. After all, these days it's difficult enough just trying to navigate down the basement stairs alone without having to hang onto and balance a basket of laundry as well. A clothes chute would sure make that job much easier.

I've tried several methods of getting the laundry down the basement steps more easily. Sometimes I'll back down the steps, one at a time, while gingerly hanging on to the handrail as I slide the basket down in front of me step by step. It's time-consuming, but does get the job done. Other times, I simply stuff everything into plastic garbage bags and toss them down ahead of me.

I've even taken to keeping a comfortable old porch chair in the basement so I can sit and read while waiting for the laundry to be done just so I don't have to make the return trip upstairs more times than necessary.

Think of it. Man has invented the microwave, frozen dinners, and instant-everything, but nothing's ever been invented that makes it easier to do laundry. For a long time now, I've heard that robots are in our future. Well, I'd sure like to know where mine is. He could be a big help when it comes to doing laundry!

Gloria Burke *has taught middle school, high school, and college English for many years, but it wasn't until she began teaching a memoir-writing class in 1992 that her own writing career took off. At age eighty-three, she continues to teach "Writing Your Memories" to adults. (419) 885-1413*

I Believe in Facebook!

by Kathe Kokolias

I admit it. I'm an old-fashioned kind of gal. Slowly and reluctantly, I embraced computer technology; it wore me down like a persistent lover who would not go away. While in graduate school, I was introduced to the word processor. In no time at all, I mastered the cut-and-paste commands and was delighted to move text instantly, thereby dashing off research papers easily.

Prior to that, I'd write my reports longhand on a yellow legal pad, cut out sections with scissors, position them on the dining room floor until they were in the right order, then tape them together into a scroll. Another method had been to type papers on my red Selectric typewriter and use carbon paper to make duplicates. Oh, how I dreaded making a typo.

With the advent of e-mail, I grudgingly admitted it had merit, although to this day I still prefer talking face to face or by phone. Snail mail, the disparaging term for what used to be the norm, is a lost art. When I turn on my laptop, I cringe to see sixty-five new messages waiting to be read; I regard them like bills demanding to be paid. I have turned off the voice message, "You've got mail." That sound alone makes me apprehensive.

Believe it or not, it was my three-year-old grandson, Zach, who first taught me how to use e-mail when we signed up years ago. After my husband and I moved to Mexico, being able to stay in touch with loved ones via e-mail minimized the pain of separation and expensive phone calls.

Then years later, Facebook, an innovative social network that allows us a means of simultaneously staying in touch with multiple people, came on the scene. My friend Karen, whom I've known since the sixth grade, would call from Manhattan for our weekly Sunday evening chats and give me reports about my grandchildren, whom she'd seen on Facebook.

"It looks like Sara had a fun time on her field trip. If you'd get on Facebook, you could see for yourself," she'd say, trying to entice me. "And you'll never guess which of our friends from Lansingburgh High I found."

"That's great, Kare," I'd reply, "but it's just not for me. Besides, why should I join when I can get all the news from you?"

Then Sara, my ten-year-old granddaughter, showed me her Facebook account and how to download photographs to share. "See how easy it is?" she said, promising to help me choose a photo for my home page. I was weakened and tempted, but still not convinced. That is, not until my phone rang late one night about eight months ago.

It was my brother, Chuck, shouting as though his cell phone had failed and he was trying to communicate with tin cans and a string.

"I found Teddy," he gushed. "Or rather, Teddy found me!"

"Slow down, Chuck. Are you talking about Teddy, your son?"

"Yes," he cried joyously. "It's a miracle!"

Yes, it most certainly was a miracle. In 1975, Chuck had married a classmate of mine from nursing school and they had had a precious son, Teddy. But when the baby was two, Chuck and his wife divorced, and from that day forward, his wife would never let any of us have contact with Teddy. Not my brother, not my father—whose heart was broken—not me, my children, nor anyone else on my side of the family. Teddy was lost to us and we mourned him as if there'd been a death in the family.

Now after thirty years, Chuck and Teddy had reconnected! Teddy—by now known as Ted—was thirty-four years old, a husband, father of two, and a helicopter pilot and lieutenant commander in the Navy. Ted had been trying to find his father for years, but it was not until Chuck joined Facebook to stay in touch with high school chums whom he'd seen at his fortieth reunion that Ted finally knew how to contact his dad.

Today is Ted's birthday, and I celebrate having him back in the family fold! So far, we've spoken by phone and exchanged e-mails, but next week, I'll be flying to Virginia Beach to actually see and hug him, meet his wife, Lauren, and his children, Sophia and Teddy. Chuck will be there celebrating too.

Well, it's no surprise that I saw the value of Facebook and quickly acquiesced, linking up with family and friends. And while it's unlikely that I'll ever be mistaken for a die-hard fan because I don't play games, join groups, or take quizzes, I do love seeing the latest photos of people I care about and getting a glimpse into their lives.

I always enjoy repeating this tale, and smile each time I come to its storybook happy ending. So now you know . . . that's why I believe in Facebook!

Kathe Kokolias *is a writer, photographer, and painter who lives in Colonie, NY, and Ixtapa, Mexico. She is the author of* What Time Do the Crocodiles Come Out?, Spandex & Black Boots, *and* A Woman's World Again. *kathekokolias@aol.com or you can visit her website: www.kathekokolias.com*

I Danced All Night

by Wynette Scalia

I recently moved into a beautiful retirement community called "The Gardens." It certainly has been a lovely place to live, with many comfortable amenities plus the nicest neighbors one could ever wish for. Also, we're real party animals!

On Halloween, we had a dress-up party that simply astonished me. Not only did it turn out to be more fun than I ever dreamed possible, but I also couldn't believe how many creative costumes abounded—everything from sexy witches to M & Ms (little round M & Ms on little round people) . . . Very innovative, very cute.

And when the time came for food and refreshments, the sky was the limit. First, we were offered any cocktail or mixed drink of our choice, both alcoholic and nonalcoholic. Then, a delicious assortment of mouth-watering hors d'oeuvres was served, which—combined with all the smiles, laughter, and cheerful conversation—was a most successful prelude to dinner. Dinner, itself, was gourmet, served with wine and elegance. And once the live combo began to play and the dancing began, the room really began to rock! Oh, what fun!

We laughed some more, we drank some more, and we danced until we were totally spent. I wandered home, weary but contented after a long night of fun . . . Wait, the hour had to be wrong . . . it was only 7:45 p.m.!!!

Wynette Scalia *loves to serve as a volunteer. She crochets, knits, travels, and enjoys playing tennis and cards with friends. Wynette also finds enjoyment exploring the internet.*

Senior Moments

by Carol Corwin Bekendam

Bill Cosby once said he believes that "memory is in one's pants," because whenever he gets up to fetch something, he invariably forgets what he went for until he sits back down again. Several years ago, I had a variation of that situation . . .

It was one of those sunny fall days in the leafy, picturesque village of Claremont, California, where I'm a psychologist in private practice. Whenever I take a lunch break I generally walk rather than drive to one of the many charming restaurants nestled between small gift shops in this quaint shopper's paradise.

But on this particular day, I needed to run an errand at a mall in a nearby town, so instead of walking, I drove my car out of its usual designated parking space in my office building parking lot. Once leaving the lot, however, I decided I'd better have lunch first right there in the village, so I quickly found a spot on Yale Street and parked. Following lunch, I checked my watch and decided I'd skip my errand and instead walk straight back to the office so I'd be on time for my next client.

That evening after work, I followed my usual routine and walked from my office to my assigned parking place, only to find my car missing! It was with astonishment and some anxiety that I called the police, who came out to take a report, promising to notify me if and when they located my car. My husband, Pete, came to pick me up.

Then at 3:00 a.m. the telephone rang. It was the Claremont Police calling to tell me they had located my car parked in downtown Claremont. So my husband and I dressed quickly and drove the short distance to the village. Yes, there was my car, looking quite lonely all by itself on the deserted street.

"Strange," said the officer, standing by my car, "it's all locked up tight and it doesn't look like anything's missing." "Yes, it is strange," I agreed. I thanked the officer and he left, as did my husband.

I unlocked the car, feeling relieved, and sat down behind the wheel. When I turned on my headlights, there in the storefront window hung the same black and white cow print pajamas I had seen at lunchtime, which jogged my memory, and then of course I remembered the moment I parked there.

As I came in the door to my house I was laughing, and my husband teased, "You forgot you parked there, didn't you?" I said, "Yes, but I'm glad I didn't remember that until *after* the police left." Pete just grumbled good-naturedly. "Okay, now let's get some sleep."

Carol Corwin Bekendam is a seventy-six-year-old clinical psychologist with a private practice in Claremont, California. She was recently inspired to write an historical novel about Moses and Hatshepsut following a trip to Egypt. She and her large family are eagerly awaiting publication of her first novel, The Prophet and the Pharaoh. *(909) 560-2005*

The Rummage Sale

by Jan Fowler

I t was time for the annual YWCA spring rummage sale, and as a
board member, this year it would be my turn to be in charge. I
was delighted. It was exactly the incentive I needed to clear my
house of clutter, especially those unwanted, outdated, and outgrown
children's games, books, toys, puzzles, and stuffed animals. With
Janelle, Kristen, and Randy all in elementary school these days, it was
hard *not* to notice how rapidly they outgrew everything. Yes, we had
plenty of quality items to donate to the sale and I knew exactly where
to begin gathering them up. In their bedrooms, of course. A single
glance at their tightly crammed bookshelves and closets revealed no
space for them to ever add anything new.

Not that *they* would see it that way, you understand; that much
I knew for sure. So I prepared myself for their inevitable resistance.
And just as predicted, when asked to clear their rooms of their worn-
out, yet beloved, possessions, they saw things a lot less enthusiastically
than me. So here's how I struck a bargain with them. (After all, wasn't
I a smart and seasoned mom who knew how to motivate?)

To sweeten their attitude and overcome objections, I promised that
on the day of the sale, I'd arrange for their dad to drive them to the Y
during the last hour when all prices would be slashed down to a dollar
a bag. Each child would be given a large brown grocery bag—my
treat—and be allowed to buy anything they wanted. Anything! Games,
books, puzzles, toys, or playthings—whatever stash their bag would
hold. Their eyes immediately brightened. Yes, they loved the idea!

It was then I explained that to create space for *new* treasures,
they'd need to clear out some old stuff. And so as I gradually won

their cooperation over the following days and weeks, I cheerfully toted boxes and bags heaped with their outdated or outgrown games, toys, dolls, balls, raggedy, faded stuffed animals, plus armloads of give-away books, to the Y as our donations to the sale.

When the day of the event finally arrived, as promised, during late afternoon their dad brought them into the large Y gymnasium, which was still heaped with clothing, assorted housewares, toys, and gardening tools. I smiled cheerfully and waved at them from across the room while still marking down numerous final items. I even blew kisses but they were much too wide-eyed and preoccupied to pay me much attention as they excitedly dashed from table to table, snatching up this and that to fill up their bags. Oh, good! I felt relieved to see them happy. They were having fun.

Later that evening after the clean-up, when I finally arrived home worn and tired, I saw all three kids laughing, cheering, and giggling while sprawled on the family room floor, legs apart with their brown paper bags between them. Suddenly something familiar caught my eye. Then another and another . . . "Mom, Mom, come see!" they grinned happily. Oh no . . . "Lordy, Lordy," I wailed, shaking my head. "What in the world? How could this be? And to think that I was such a smart mom!"

By now, of course, you've guessed the truth. Yes, Janelle, Kristen, and Randy had each bought back *every single possession* they could find that once belonged to them and that I'd forced them to give away to the annual YWCA rummage sale!

Jan Fowler is an award-winning columnist, television producer/host, and national speaker on senior topics. She developed a passion for the senior population during her long career as a licensed speech pathologist and is now an ambassador for seniors everywhere. Jan has five grandchildren and lives in southern California. She is the founder of Starburst Inspirations nonprofit corporation and is a member of National League of American Pen Women. www.janfowler.com or janfowlerusa@yahoo.com

A Matter of Style

by Cheryl McFadden

These days, it seems that all I have to do to prepare for an evening out on the town is to slide my bare feet into clogs, slip on a pair of jeans, a turtleneck sweater, and leather jacket. Now if I *really* want to gussy up my outfit, I'll dig out my hoop earrings.

Style in the twenty-first century is so open to interpretation. How things have changed since the early '50s when my mother got ready to go out and paint the town! She was an extremely attractive single woman, intent upon dazzling her suitors, but no one was more impressed than I.

Lying on my stomach on her bed with my chin cupped in my upturned hands, I studied my mother intently as the ritual began.

First came the Merry Widow, which made her trim figure look so curvy and alluring. The apparatus had to be uncomfortable with all that squeezing, pushing, cinching, and clinching, but I thought it was the height of glamour. I could hardly wait till I had something of my own that could be squeezed, pushed, cinched, and clinched.

Totally captivated, I declared, "When I grow up, I want to be just as beautiful as you!"

Continuing with the process, she perched herself on the edge of the bed and bewitchingly inserted each leg into a nylon stocking. Each was then fastened in place with a garter, all the while exposing smooth white flesh at the thigh—a tantalizing hint of the mystery of sex that awaited me in grown-up years. Next she glided a delicate silk slip over her body, carefully smoothing it into place before stepping into her dress of choice. She had many beautiful dresses, but my favorites were the taffeta dresses that whooshed and rustled with every step.

When I was finally old enough to wear the clothes that had intrigued me as a child, alas, they were no longer in style. In the late '60s women were beginning to burn their bras. Comfort had replaced elegance. My underwear did not consist of corsets and garters. Pantyhose had arrived. (Hallelujah!) A very good thing indeed, since the hems were above where the imagination left off.

Miniskirts ruled and I loved showing off my long legs, accentuating them even further with shiny vinyl knee-high boots. Those boots were made for walking, or more accurately, strutting. Polyester in every wild psychedelic color imaginable dominated fashion. It was the Age of Aquarius and I wore flowers in my ironed hair and on my clothes; I even stuck them on my car. Groovy!

Fashions have come and gone over the years, but none stands out in my memory as much as those worn by my mother during the '50s and me during the '60s.

"Anything goes," seems to be the modern anthem, with an emphasis on casual. Actually, that's all right with me. Some things, such as corsets and nylons, are better suited to memories. My only decision for tonight is—should I wear Wranglers or Levis?

Cheryl McFadden *discovered that she was a writer shortly after retiring. Most of her writing is devoted to a monthly newsletter she created and maintains. Since photography is also among her passions, she combines both interests whenever possible.* CMCFAD9739@aol.com

It's Still a Good Run

by Gloria Burke

Now that I am in my eighth decade, I'm beginning to recognize a few increasing infirmities that I wish I could ignore. For example, just the short trip from my Lazy Girl chair to the kitchen is beginning to leave me feeling tuckered out.

I recall how when I was in my late fifties I had packed up and moved from Ohio to Arizona. For the previous ten years I'd been teaching problem teenagers in an alternative high school. These were kids who were addicted to drugs, having trouble with the law, and who were seriously lacking in academic credits. They were sent to an off-campus location in hopes that small classes and more individualized attention would help motivate them to turn their young lives around.

But as it turned out, the more I worked with them, the more I realized that *my* life was the one that needed turning around. After twenty-six years of marriage, I found myself divorced. Since I blamed myself so much for the breakup, I even refused to accept financial support from my ex-husband. It was a gutsy move, but I was determined to forge ahead on my own steam. So I moved from the Midwest and settled in Mesa, Arizona, where I first began working as a substitute teacher in area schools, then later taught English and journalism at a middle school.

Back in the thirties and forties, dramatic readings had been a popular form of entertainment for social gatherings, and since my mother had been a frequent performer in little theater and was also a dramatic reader, she taught me how to memorize monologues. It wasn't long before she and I began entertaining as a duo. I was only six years old.

So one day when I saw a casting call in the *Mesa Tribune* for auditions at Mesa Little Theatre, it seemed like a natural fit for me. I attended auditions, was cast in a play, and acting soon opened up a new Southwest lifestyle that agreed with me. I taught during the day and filled my evenings and weekends with the fun of rehearsals, memorizing lines, and performing on stage.

In 1989, however, when I learned that my daughter was expecting a baby, I decided to return to the Midwest. Once back home, I began teaching computer-assisted English at a local two-year college. Macintosh was the "in" computer in those days and I knew nothing about it. But I landed the job and was soon navigating my way around the "Mac" like an old pro. It wasn't the first time I'd gotten a job through the "back door."

Traveling in the slow lane is more my speed now, but the brain is still running full speed ahead. I now coordinate an ongoing learning program for men and women over fifty.

There've been lots of good, bad, and "in-betweens" in these eighty years, but it's still a good run, and I'll take as much more of it as I can get!

Gloria Burke ~ *It wasn't until Gloria began teaching a "Writing Your Memories" class for adults in 1992 that her own writing career took off. She has taught English classes at the middle school, high school, and college levels for many years, and at eighty-three, she still works. (419) 885-1413*

Growing Up

by Barbara Whitehead

I don't jump out of bed too quickly like I used to do before,
 My body feels a shockeroo when my tootsies hit the floor,
I bend and stretch and stretch again as high as I can go,
 The little aches and pains take hold from my hair down
 to my toe.

I brush my teeth and thank the Lord that every tooth is mine,
 The face in the mirror is slightly blurred, but with glasses,
 it's just fine.
There are wrinkles by my eyes these days—"character lines,"
 I'm told,
 And the silver in my tresses has long replaced the gold.

I walk a little slower now, which is really quite okay,
 It gives me time to pick the flowers that grow along
 the way,
I've paid my dues through all these years, and if I may be so
 bold
 I will admit I'm growing up, but *never* growing old.

Emotions change from day to day—it's how I cope that
 matters,
 It's how I hold my chin up when the world around me
 shatters,
Hurtful words still make me cry as they did in years before,
 Tears can flow as easily whether you're six or sixty-four.

But I've learned a little trick for when things go from bad to
worse,
I pull out pen and paper and write a little verse.
It's easier not to rant and rave—it's sure better than being
delirious.
It works for me, folks, all the time 'cause life is not that
serious.

I find it hard to kneel too long when the moment comes for
prayer,
But since I've known my God so long, He accepts me in my
chair.

We sit and chat, we "shoot the breeze," we while away the
hours.
I thank Him for the gifts He gives . . . for sunshine and the
showers.

When I was young and not so wise, my prayers were always
the same.
Asking for something every time I called upon His name.
It was "Give me this, Lord, give me that, please tell me
what to do."
But in my old age I ask no more—I *know* He'll see me
through.

I know the time is coming soon for that "closer walk with
Thee,"
It's been a little while, dear Lord, since I sat upon your knee.
I have one last prayer for that final day when my soul is
cleansed from sin.
Please open up those pearly gates, saying, "Barbara, come
right in!"

Barbara Whitehead *is a retired businesswomen and mother of six. She and her husband, William, live in the foothills of the Sierras where she is fulfilling her life's dream of living life as a "country girl." (559) 641-7773*

Chapter 14:
WORDS OF PEARLY WISDOM

When All You've Ever Wanted Isn't Enough

by Harold Kushner

I remember reading an interview once with an eighty-five-year-old woman from the hill country of Kentucky, who was asked to look back over her life and reflect on what she had learned. With that touch of wistfulness that inevitably accompanies any statement beginning "If I had it to do over . . . ," she said, "If I had my life to live over, I would dare to make more mistakes next time. I would relax. I would be sillier, I would take fewer things seriously . . .

"I would eat more ice cream and less beans. I would perhaps have more actual troubles but fewer imaginary ones. You see, I'm one of those people who lived seriously and sanely hour after hour, day after day. I've been one of those persons who never went anyplace without a thermometer, a hot water bottle, a raincoat, and a parachute. If I had it to do again, I'd travel lighter."

The woman from Kentucky feels that she has wasted too much of her life following the wrong advice and wants to keep us from making the same mistake. She has come to understand how easily the pleasures of life today are spoiled by worry about what might happen tomorrow. She has learned how fear can banish joy, making us tense with apprehension, and how laughter can chase fear and set us free. And she wants to pass those lessons on to us.

Reprinted from When All You've Ever Wanted Isn't Enough with the kind permission of author **Harold Kushner,** copyright owner.

Harold Kushner *is Rabbi Laureate of Temple Israel, Natick, Massachusetts. He is also the author of numerous inspiring and consoling books, including the international bestseller* When Bad Things Happen to Good People, *which was written after his son Aaron died from the premature aging disease, Progeria. Kushner was given the Lifetime Achievement Award by the Jewish Book Council in 2007.*

Money

by Byron Katie

I love having money, and I love not having it. To me, spending money is nothing more than passing on what didn't belong to me in the first place. There's nothing I can do to keep it away, as long as it needs to be passed on. If it doesn't need to be passed on, there's no need for it to come. I love that it comes in, and I love that it goes out.

When I receive money, I am thrilled, because I'm fully aware that it's not mine. I'm just a channel, I'm not even the caretaker. I get to be the observer of it, to see what it's for. The moment I get it from over there, a need for it pops up over here. I love giving money. I never lend people money; I *give* them money, and they call it a loan. If they repay it, that's when I know it was a loan.

Used by permission of Harmony Books, a division of Random House, Inc. From *A Thousand Names for Joy: Living in Harmony with the Way Things Are* by **Byron Katie** with Stephen Mitchell, copyright © 2007 by Byron Kathleen Mitchell.

Byron Katie is widely recognized for her method of self-inquiry known as "The Work". She has written three bestselling books and has helped millions of people across the world begin to end their suffering. Her website is www.thework.com, *where you will find many free materials to download, as well as audio and video clips, a schedule of events, and a free helpline with a network of Work facilitators.*

The Story of the Queen Bee

by Barbara A. Berg

One day, a few years ago, a customer came in to see Judy at the bank where she worked as a loan officer. As they were going over possible options for loans, Judy asked this industrious young man, Rick, "What exactly do you do for a living?" Rick smiled and said, "I'm a bee keeper."

Being pretty much a city girl, Judy said, "What exactly does a bee keeper do?" Patiently, Rick explained to her that he takes bee hives in his truck to various farms to have them cross-pollinate.

Rick went on to say that he places the bee hives in such a way that the bees leave their hive and go from tree to tree, thus cross-pollinating. When Judy asked, "How do you get the bees to go back to the hive?" Rick was surprised Judy didn't know. He said "Why, they come back to the hive because the Queen Bee is there!" *He had Judy's attention.*

She then asked in amazement, "What does the Queen Bee do all day?" Still being patient but again surprised that Judy didn't know, he simply said, "She sits!" Finding it hard to imagine herself ever sitting still, never mind a bee, Judy went on to ask, "Does the Queen Bee ever try to help?" Rick said, "Yes, once in a great while. But if she does, the worker bees won't come back to her. They won't recognize her as the Queen. They'll see her as a worker bee, just like them."

He then added, probably for his own edification as much as trying to answer Judy's questions even before she asked, "Generally speaking, the Queen Bee sits because she *has* and *is* everything she needs to be. She just knows the other bees will come back to her. She knows that whatever she needs will come to her without any effort of her own. That *knowing* is what brings them back."

Judy chimed in, mainly with admiration for the Queen Bee and a little tinge of sarcasm, "I guess she just knows her self-worth." Nodding in some sort of agreement, but not with the same intensity of emotion invested as Judy seemed to have, Rick added, "Come to think of it, my entire business depends on the Queen Bee knowing her self-worth."

Sitting there staring at Rick for what was probably longer than is customary for a loan officer to do in front of a potential client, Judy finally heard Rick say he had to get back to his truck. His bees were in the hives in cages in the back, and he had a farm to get to. He shook Judy's hand while she was still sitting—it was probably the stillest she had sat for a long time—thanked her for her time, and took the brochures from the bank.

Ever since then, Judy began asking her boyfriend for what she needed from him in a positive and pleasant way. She came to see that if this guy didn't come through, she would learn more about whether he was the right man for her. She also realized that hearing herself ask was the important part. Soon Judy became willing to sit still and wait for the right man to appear, *knowing* she needn't settle for just anyone in order to be with someone anymore.

From *Ring Shui* with the kind permission of author **Barbara Cowan Berg**.

Barbara A. Berg is a popular keynote speaker, radio and television guest, psychotherapist, and the author of How to Escape the No-Win Trap *and* What To Do When Life is Driving You Crazy! *barbaraberg. com*

Letter to Page

by Phyllis Costello

Dear Page,

*Y*ou sounded scared in your e-mail, but I know that what I'm about to say will calm your fears.

I was born in the middle of the last "Great Depression." Living in those desperate times was not easy, but people survived. Families moved in with one another. Men walked the streets looking for work. Women cut corners at home.

Food was simple. My dad loved navy beans and corn bread. We didn't use ham in the beans; it was bacon. At times, it could even be beans and white bread. My aunt loved corn on the cob and we had whole meals that consisted of sweet corn. Meatloaf was prepared with a great deal of filler. We ate lots of noodles and potatoes; they fill people up. Everyone raised large gardens and canned fruits and vegetables for the coming winter. Pot roasts and chicken were saved for Sunday dinner.

We cleaned our own houses and mowed our own lawns. We stayed home together, playing cards and a few board games. Clothing was passed around until it became threadbare, then was patched. Shoes were worn until they had holes in the soles. Cardboard placed inside the shoe covered the hole. Sometimes a winter coat had to be shared—one person going out and the other staying home.

My mother bought drapes for the living room from Woolworth's. The dime store felt magical with the variety of goods. Grandma made slip covers on the sewing machine. Mama braided rugs from old ties and worn-out clothes.

Christmas gifts were homemade and only one gift per person. Toys were often painted and redone. Christmas trees were small with homemade decorations by the kids. The spindly little tree was the only decoration in the house, but kids were just as excited then as now. Magically, moms somehow managed to squeeze out holiday dinner with turkey and pie. So Christmas became the highlight of the year.

It's best not to waste anything, whether it's food or money. Mother always shared what we had with tramps who came knocking on the door. She not only fed them, but also sent food for them to take on the road. Today, they would be called homeless. We always had time and food to share with anyone. It was a time of loving and caring.

I learned a lot about the value of money.

Warren Buffet, the world's richest man, just gave away 350 billion dollars. His advice, "Live simply. Don't waste your money on unnecessary things. Rather, spend on those really in need. The happiest people do not necessarily have the best of all things. They simply appreciate what they find on their way." He lives his own advice.

Many adults look back with a yearning to experience those times again.

Honey, you will make it through the present hard times and learn much about life. You are young. You are strong. You are caring. You have a family that loves you.

Your loving aunt,
Madelyn

Phyllis Costello (posthumously) was multitalented and loved to teach metaphysical truths. She walked her talk, believing that life always presents the best to you if you expect it to. Phyllis enjoyed her life right up to the end. She stayed actively involved in her local writers' guild, had a "firecracker personality," and mostly loved to make people laugh.

Find Your Magic Star

by John Gray, Ph.D.

I remember when my daughter Lauren first learned about the magic of asking for what you want and having faith. When she was about five years old, we were on vacation in Hawaii. She found a box of "magic stars" in a little bookstore. She picked one up and asked me what it was. I took one and read the instructions, which said something like this: "Hold this magic star close to your heart, close your eyes, and then make a wish. You can have anything you want."

When she heard this she lit up with such excitement. It was as if she had made the discovery of a lifetime. She said, "Can I ask for anything?" I said yes. She asked if I would get her one. As we were walking along the beach, she was beaming with a huge smile. She was so happy. She was holding her magic star next to her heart and making wishes. This was just the coolest thing she could imagine.

Then after a few hours, she asked, "Daddy, how come my wishes aren't coming true?" I thought, "Oh God, how can I answer this?" Well, I didn't have to. My wife, Bonnie, responded by saying, "As long as you keep your heart open and continue to make your wishes, then they will come true. But they don't always come true right away. It takes time, and you have to have patience." Lauren was satisfied with this answer, and she continued to beam.

In that one statement, Bonnie had summarized the secret of outer success, which is probably why she has so much in her life: Keep your heart open and continue to want what you want. This secret explains why so many people lose their creative power. When they don't get what they want, they give up and stop believing. The secret of creating is sustaining a strong, willful intention. It feels like this: "I will have that, I really want it, and I trust that it will come." In this way, desire and trust turn into a strong, willful intention.

Knowing What You Really Want

By getting in touch and staying in touch with your deepest desires, you can find your own magic star. By continuing to focus and feel what you really want, you will increase your power to create your life. First in your mind and heart and then through your actions, you will be increasingly successful in creating what you really want.

Knowing what you really want is not as easy as it sounds. There are many ways we get distracted from our true desires. Sometimes it is just too painful to feel what we really want, and we believe that we will never have it. Fear is one of the major reasons we don't give ourselves permission to feel what we want. If we want something that is not as important to us and we don't get it, it's not so painful. If we let ourselves really feel what is most important to us, it may be too painful to fail.

When I began giving public talks twenty-eight years ago, I felt tremendous anxiety and fear. I felt most nervous about speaking because that was one of my gifts in life, what I came here to do. If I failed at speaking, I would be devastated. If I failed as a computer programmer, it would not be so crushing because my gift was not programming. That was not my purpose in life.

Whenever you risk doing that which is closer to who you are, the thought of rejection or failure is greater. It is one thing to be rejected by others for the clothes you wear; it is an entirely different story to be rejected for your beliefs. When you are true to who you are, you are exposed. If you are rejected or criticized, then it cuts much closer and it hurts more.

Trust, Caring, and Desire

When we have a desire that is not fulfilled, quite commonly we give it up in some way. We stop caring as much, we stop wanting, we stop trusting. When a man stops believing, he will stop caring. When a woman stops believing, she will tend to stop trusting. In both cases, they will give up hope. Hope is vitally important to stay in touch with our ability to feel our desires fully.

Trust, caring, and strong desire are the ingredients of power. We need all three.

[Reprinted by permission of HarperCollins Publishers from *How to Get What You Want and Want What You Have* by **John Gray**. Copyright © 1998 by Mars Productions, Inc.]

John Gray, Ph.D. *is a family and relationship therapist, author, teacher, and speaker. He has written seventeen books dealing with personal growth, love, romance, and communication, and is best known for* Men Are from Mars, Women Are from Venus. *www.marsvenus.com*

"Seniorless" Seniors

by Andrea Giambrone

Here we are, roughly forty million of us who are sixty-five or older. It's a wonder that we don't hear a giant collective groan when we bend down to pick up something. Maybe it's because we're smart enough to either *not* bend down or are in the kind of shape that our parents and grandparents would have marveled at, unless you happen to be the offspring of Jack LaLanne.

A lot of seniors I know take really good care of themselves. Far from any Norman Rockwell drawing of white-haired people in aprons and overalls, the majority of my friends are into yoga, swimming, sex (hey, I don't ask for details; I only know they're not lying), mountain climbing, parachute jumping (better than me), starting businesses, or doing volunteer work that goes to the heart of what it is to be a senior.

Many of us seem more fearless than we used to be. Why not? After all, what do we have to lose? We have loads of experience. I would love to believe that the wonderful euphemistic term "we're seasoned" means that we've had lots of salt and pepper liberally lavished upon us. A "seasoned veteran" is what I became, quite automatically, when I stayed at the same company for almost thirty years. And goodness knows I can be plenty salty.

We have a storehouse of cherished memories from when people spent money sensibly, didn't buy what they couldn't afford, remembered to "do unto others," and other old-fashioned notions that strike us as extraordinarily sound during these economic meltdown days.

We share one very basic secret. We really believe we will die. Hardly morbid. It actually frees us to do whatever we want to do now. My seriously older friends (in their 90s) are genuinely living their lives to the fullest. One man manages his considerable investments online; another goes to more theater performances and restaurants in a month than most of us do in a year. Oh, and at the age of ninety-one, he has a lady friend who, at seventy-seven, is gorgeous. They fell in love a few years ago and have been as happy as the clams they can eat by the dozen.

Good genes absolutely have a lot to do with it. And a great attitude also seems to be the backbone of living and aging well. As when my brother-in-law, whose sense of humor has served him well throughout his seventy-two years, told me that the epitaph he thought best suited him are the words, "I knew this would happen."

We don't kid ourselves into believing we're immortal. We know better, so we milk it for all it's worth. Our esteemed author, Jan Fowler, is a perfect example. By definition a senior, she's revamped her life in recent years to include hosting a talk show, writing a column, and now this book.

Perhaps we're best described as the "seniorless seniors." We fit the Social Security description plus the census statistics of us, but we're redefining what "older" means by being vibrant, involved, dynamic, and a whole lot surer of ourselves than any twenty-something will ever be.

We really have been there, done that! And, though we might not be ready to kick up our heels as high, or dance as long as those younger than we, our collective juicing of life makes for a rocket-booster cocktail.

So to my "seniorless" brothers and sisters . . . Salud!

Andrea Giambrone *has had a lifelong love affair with writing, and is a professional speaker, columnist, advertising writer, and published poet. As freelance consultant and president of her own advertising service, Think a la Carte, Andrea is the supreme and consummate wordsmith. www.thinkalacarte.com or ag@thinkalacarte.com*

Your Problem is a Gift

by Barbara A. Berg

There is a "gift" in every situation and every interaction we ever have. Some of these gifts come as people and situations that make it easier to love ourselves, whereas some just seem to make it harder. The purpose of these gifts is to help us see whether it's best to move closer to another person with all our heart and energy, or move away and be loving from a more detached position.

Whichever dilemma you're in right now is a gift. View it from as many perspectives as you can, then choose the route that most benefits you and others in the long run. Leave the no-win traps behind; they'll always be there for those who want to sign up.

Only you can choose what to do in this moment. Choose a thought that will bring you peace and freedom. Perhaps you'll choose to forgive, perhaps you'll let go, perhaps you'll choose to view that situation from another person's point of view. Whichever, choose to believe that your needs will be met and that the process is already happening. Always stay focused on living a life that reflects who you truly are.

From *How to Escape the No-Win Trap* with the kind permission of author **Barbara Cowan Berg**.

Barbara Berg is a popular keynote speaker, radio and television guest, psychotherapist, and the author of What To Do When Life is Driving You Crazy! *and* Ring Shui.

Senior Savvy

by Jan Fowler

Things work out for the best for those who make the best of the way things work out.

Abe Lincoln

S orry, I can't reveal *all* my secrets because you know what they say in spy movies. "If I tell you, then I may have to kill you." But I'm happy to share a few of my favorite nuggets—the ones that work best for me and have shaped my overall outlook and attitude. (After all, surely there must be *some* gems to show for the years spent accumulating grays, wrinkles, and cellulite.) So here goes . . .

- The seven deadly sins—*pride, anger, envy, greed, gluttony, lust, and sloth*—still pretty much cover it all. Avoid them whenever you can.
- Nothing makes as much sense as common sense.
- Life is measured more in spirit and outlook than in years, so stay young-at-heart.
- Mother was right—a smile may be your best asset.
- Avoid portion-distortion like the plague.
- Don't "over-think" problems. Instead, dive into solutions.
- Rebound from failure—the faster the better! Even when you don't win, you always learn more about yourself by going through the process. Sometimes a minor stall is exactly what's needed to take a giant step forward.

- Remain open to new experiences such as untried music, food, art, and diverse people. Learn a new skill, dance, or sport; take a class, watch a new channel, take a new route home. Always keep an open mind.
- Exercise regularly. Increase your workout sessions by just five minutes, and walk rather than drive.
- Make notes as memory aids.
- Make others laugh. Try to become their answer to prayer by improving their circumstances or quality of life. Doing so fills the empty spaces in your heart.
- Be joyful. A good attitude is a great thing to have. It makes people want to be with you. Positive emotions have a positive effect upon heart health and longevity, so prescribe smiles, fun, and happy times for yourself. Seek out others who are cheerful, upbeat, sunny, and rosy. Avoid grouches whenever possible.
- Be a playful player in the overall game of life! And by the way, a positive attitude doesn't just happen—you may have to work at learning to laugh more, but it's worth training yourself to be happy and hopeful. Besides which, you increase your chances of living a longer, more productive life. So use bravado if that's what it takes to get you going.
- And above all, *always always always* do your best to bring sunshine into the lives of others!

Jan Fowler is an award-winning columnist, television producer/ host, and national speaker on senior topics. She developed a passion for the senior population during her long career as a licensed speech pathologist and is now an ambassador for seniors everywhere. Jan has five grandchildren and lives in southern California. She is the founder of Starburst Inspirations nonprofit corporation and is a member of the National League of American Pen Women. www.janfowler.com or janfowlerusa@yahoo.com

ABOUT THE AUTHOR

Jan Fowler is an award-winning columnist, television producer/host and national speaker on senior topics. She developed a passion for the senior population during her long career as a licensed speech pathologist, has written two speech therapy books, and has become an ambassador for seniors everywhere.

She is the founder of Starburst Inspirations, her community service award-winning 501 (c) (3) nonprofit corporation that recognizes and supports the work of Drug Court.

Jan is also a community theatre actress, emcee, philanthropist, and popular speaker at Senior Expos and events.

She was one of ten Inland Empire, CA women to receive the Town & Gown "Phenomenal Women" award (2005) and was twice the recipient of the "Woman of Achievement" award from the National League of American Pen Women. Jan has five grandchildren and lives in southern California.

www.janfowler.com
Order from Jan Fowler Senior Productions
1554 Barton Rd., Suite 251, Redlands, CA 92373
(909) 793-6419

CPSIA information can be obtained at www.ICGtesting.com
Printed in the USA
LVOW110936191111

255729LV00006BB/36/P